PROCESS-RELATIONAL PHILOSOPHY

Process-Relational Philosophy

AN INTRODUCTION TO
ALFRED NORTH WHITEHEAD

C. Robert Mesle

TEMPLETON FOUNDATION PRESS
WEST CONSHOHOCKEN, PENNSYLVANIA

Templeton Foundation Press
300 Conshohocken State Road, Suite 670
West Conshohocken, PA 19428 • www.templetonpress.org

Designed and typeset by Gopa and Ted2, Inc.

Printed in the United States of America

Templeton Foundation Press helps intellectual leaders and others learn about science research on aspects of realities, invisible and intangible. Spiritual realities include unlimited love, accelerating creativity, worship, and the benefits of purpose in persons and in the cosmos.

Library of Congress Cataloging-in-Publication Data

Mesle, C. Robert.
Process-relational philosophy : an introduction to Alfred North Whitehead / C. Robert Mesle.
p. cm.
Includes bibliographical references and index.
ISBN-13: 978-1-59947-132-7 (pbk. : alk. paper)
ISBN-10: 1-59947-132-9 (pbk. : alk. paper) 1. Process philosophy. 2. Relation (Philosophy) 3. Reality. I. Title.
BD372.M47 2007
146'.7—dc22

2007017844

08 09 10 11 12 13 10 9 8 7 6 5 4 3 2 1

To Elliot, who is the becoming of our future. May he have a long and wonderful journey, filled with chocolate and love.

Contents

Being and Becoming

A PERSONAL PREFACE

The secret of life is enjoying the passing of time.
—JAMES TAYLOR

IN THE EVENING, we walked on the beach. The ocean waves washed our feet in the ancient sacrament of time. In, out. In, out. Each distinct wave that touched us returned to the ocean of which it had always been a part. In, out. In, out. Yet, even the ocean itself never remains unchanged. In, out. In, out. Separate, rejoin. Become, perish.

Being and Becoming. Each points to something true, to something we care about. Every great philosophy and religion must address these fundamental categories. How shall we hold them together? Which, if either, is deeper?

Shadows, wind, and clouds pass so quickly that they seem mostly unreal. So, time and Becoming seem unreal to us. Rocks, iron, and mountains suggest unchanging reality—Being. We can count on them to last, to be there tomorrow and next year. More importantly, we don't want to die, and we know that change brings death. Only in changeless eternity can we hope to escape our mortality.

Plato gave priority to Being partly because he loved ideas. For him and so many others, the truths of mathematics provided the paradigm of reality. Circleness, squareness, and $2 + 2 = 4$ are timeless. They do not rust or wither, wear down, or fade away. You can count on them to never, ever, change—not even a little. They do not become or perish; they just are. Alfred North Whitehead was a mathematician and shared much of Plato's desire to incorporate Being into his vision of

Becoming. But mathematical forms, however important and wonderful, are abstractions. They are not actual. Whitehead argued that even in the Divine, the timeless by itself, without the temporal, is not fully actual.

Barbara, Mark and Abbey, Sarah and Brandon, our new grandson Elliot, and all the other people I love *are* actual. That means they change. As much as I love ideas, they cannot hold a candle to the people I love. I know I can count on those people, but I count on them in the ways one can and must count on all that is actual. My counting on them is all bound up with counting on them to act, grow, change, and—sadly—to perish.

Life is change. I remember Sarah, now thirty, when she was five. What a joy it was to hold her on my lap then—to hug her, read to her, and tickle her. I will never again be able to hold the five-year-old Sarah on my lap. But that is the price I must pay to have the thirty-year-old Sarah be married to Brandon and give birth to Elliot. I will never again teach the six-year-old Mark to swim, but that is what must happen for the twenty-five-year-old Mark to be living in Argentina with Abbey, making me laugh out loud with his travel blog. Life simply is change—becoming and perishing. The joy of life is in the journey.

I am a process-relational philosopher because everything I care about is in process and in relationships—even my ideas. Being part of an allegedly timeless reality holds no allure for me. Whatever people may dream or speculate regarding timeless, changeless, becomingless eternity, it is clear to me that nothing in our actual lives fits that category. I respect philosophies of Being because I understand why they speak to us in our confrontation with change, old age, and death. But I am still going to die. I believe the testimony of those who report mystical and meditative experiences they can only describe as timeless, but I know those experiences happen and then fade. I understand that in timeless eternity I would suffer no injuries, fear no diseases, feel no pain, commit no sins, experience no aging, and face no death. But what sense does it make to speak of "I" then? Hindus and Buddhists recognize that "I" would simply disappear, merging with the eternal ocean of Being. I certainly agree that, whatever I am, I am never truly separate from the larger relational whole extending infinitely in time and that my "self" will eventually be lost as I fully melt back into earth, air, fire, and water. But in a timeless eternity, if there be such, I could not hug my children, tickle Elliot, make love to my wife, or walk the beach with waves washing my feet. Even the ocean changes constantly. But just as importantly, I am committed to Becoming because everything I care about lives in time. That is why I am a process philosopher. The joy of life is in the journey.

My thanks to John B. Cobb Jr. and Herman Greene for asking me to write this little book and for their valuable and extensive comments. I also received helpful comments from John Sweeney, Les Muray, Randy Auxier, and others. The students in my Process Philosophy and Theology class of 2005 helped field test the manuscript, and the students in my 2007 class helped proofread it. My student assistant, Zoe Naylor did most of the work on the index. Always, I must thank my family for making life and work worthwhile, especially Barbara, who inspires all the good I do.

PROCESS-RELATIONAL PHILOSOPHY

1 A Process-Relational World

AN ADVENTURE THAT MATTERS

Rationalism never shakes off its status of an experimental adventure. . . . Rationalism is an adventure in the clarification of thought, progressive and never final. But it is an adventure in which even partial success has importance.

—ALFRED NORTH WHITEHEAD, *PROCESS AND REALITY*[1]

IDEAS SHAPE ACTIONS, so it matters how we think about reality, the world, and ourselves. I don't mean that only people who believe in one particular religion or philosophy can be good or intelligent people. But, clearly, it does matter how we think about the world. I want to begin by suggesting three reasons why you might want to learn more about process-relational thought. The first is simply wonder—the philosopher's joy in wondering about this incredible, amazing world. Second, thinking of the world as deeply interwoven—as an ever-renewing relational process —can change the way we feel and act. Finally, we need a coherent vision of our world, something that can engage people from many different scientific, cultural, philosophical, and religious perspectives.

The primary purpose of this book is to provide a basic introduction to the process-relational philosophy inspired principally by Alfred North Whitehead (1861–1947), especially as expressed in his seminal 1929 work *Process and Reality*. This will not be a neutral introduction. I want to persuade you that process-relational philosophy is a vision that matters, that is worth taking seriously, even as it will inevitably require us to criticize, improve, and, in some respects, transcend it. Process-relational thinking has a long history stretching back at least to the Buddha and the ancient Greek philosopher Heraclitus in the sixth century BCE. While there are many contemporary forms of process-relational thought, Whitehead provides one particularly clear and focused vision of reality shared by many people and groups around the world.

Unfortunately, Whitehead was developing his profoundly new vision of the world just as Anglo-American philosophers were throwing out the metaphysical baby with the bath water. Understandably, they found many metaphysical questions and answers to be empty and useless—literally meaningless. Yet, the need for a comprehensive vision of reality has only grown greater since Whitehead first introduced this philosophy. With the dramatic growth of science in every corner, the great emergence of ecological awareness, the explosion of thought about religious diversity, and both increased conflict and increased dialogue between science and religion, we need more than ever to find ways of thinking that can pull these many conversations together in meaningful ways. This book reflects the convictions of a network of people who believe that process-relational thought can provide such a unifying vision.

PROCESS, TIME, AND WONDER

An artist friend of mine observed that great art can make us simultaneously cry out, "Holy Cow!" and "Of course!" Great art can make us see something in a radically new way, while at the same time helping us to see that this new vision fits, that it feels right.[2] My goal in this little book is to offer a philosophical vision of reality, and of human existence in the world that makes you say both "Holy Cow!" and "Of course!" So far as I succeed, things will snap into place so that you say, "It's so obvious. Why didn't I see that before? That is how I always experienced the world, but I never knew how to say it."

Whitehead's *Process and Reality* is a very tough book, so as a graduate student thirty years ago, I took a break and walked over to Lake Michigan, trying to understand what "process" was all about. The weather was gray and the lake, choppy. "What is the alternative?" I asked myself. What if the world were not in process? Would Lake

Michigan somehow be sitting there waveless in the future, waiting for waves to break on it? Suddenly, the world jolted, as if it had been ajar and unexpectedly dropped into place with a snap.

The future does not exist. There is no future Lake Michigan waiting for water to fill it or waves to lap at its shores. The future does not exist.[3] I looked at the world around me with wide, amazed eyes. My eyes did not exist in the future. The sidewalk did not exist in the future. The foot that I was going to set down on the sidewalk in a moment did not exist yet: Only the foot in the present existed. I practically skipped home, watching the sidewalk and my feet (and my watching itself) *become*. At Morry's Deli, I looked in the window (becoming) and watched the pastrami becoming, and the people becoming.

When I returned to my third-floor apartment, I looked down into the yard next door and had a sense of vertigo. Time is like falling, I thought. We are always on the verge of falling forward into nothingness; but, in each moment, the world becomes anew, and the creative advance continues.

How could I explain this to my wife? I put a record on the player. (Yes, this was many years ago, but the image will work just as well with a CD.) Our traditional Christian view of time assumes that the future exists very much like music on a record or CD. All the "music" is stamped simultaneously onto the plastic—Pssst! The needle or laser reads the grooves and dips so that music leaps up as if it were becoming. But every note is already there, beginning, middle, and end. From the perspective of the disc, nothing new happens. The future already exists on a record or a CD.

Consider the idea that the future already exists from the perspective of the Christian theology that has so profoundly shaped Western thought. Christians have traditionally believed in an omnipotent, omniscient God who creates "time" but stands outside of time as we stand outside of a CD. Or, to pick a more traditional image, time has been seen as like a great tapestry woven by God. The tapestry tells a story, but the whole story from beginning to end exists at once on the tapestry. God, it has been assumed, is able to stand back and see the whole tapestry at once. Thus, the future may be unknown to us, but it exists—is already fully actual—for God. This concept explains how prophets are usually thought to see the future: God simply lifts them up above the tapestry so that they can see as far ahead as God chooses, because the future already exists.

Consider the image of time as a great novel. The novel has a beginning, a middle, and an end. Within the novel, people live and die, great battles are fought, and you and I agonize over decisions. Yet, none of the characters in the novel has anything to say about what they decide. That is all determined by the author. On page 73, you may be struggling with whether to marry or live in celibacy. Turning to page 76, we see what you decide. Turning back to page 40, we can read where you first met the person you love. The novelist has created it all, and having been created, the past, present, and future are all fully settled, fully actually, fully achieved simultaneously. Since God, as the novelist, is outside of time, outside of the novel, there is not even a process of creation for God. God is timelessly eternal, with no past or future. So the novel exists timelessly in the mind of God—static, unchanging, eternal—with every decision, every action determined totally by the divine Author.

This static view of time in which the future already exists explains why Christians often assume that everything is predetermined by God. Obviously, if God created the tapestry of time, with the whole world story on it, we had and have nothing to say about what God decided we would do. Whatever is going to happen has already happened. When did God create time? Since God is outside of time, the answer can only be something like "timelessly" or "eternally." So, whatever is going to happen in the future actually happens eternally.

Western thinkers have generally avoided the Eastern view that time and change are illusions, though Parmenides proposed a similar view about twenty-five centuries ago. Still, you can see that in important ways Western Christians have said that time is a kind of illusion. From God's perspective, which surely defines ultimate reality, nothing new happens, nothing changes. God is eternal, and so is the world. Being is real, but Becoming is a kind of illusion experienced only by us finite creatures trapped within time. In this and other ways, the philosophy of Being rather than Becoming has dominated Western thought.

The view of time in which the past, present, and future exist simultaneously, so that the future already and always exists—is already fully settled and actual—is exactly the view of time that I threw aside when I discovered that the future does not exist and became a process philosopher. *The future does not exist.* There isn't even a future "out there" waiting to happen. Decisions must be made; the future must be created. The creatures of the present must decide between many possibilities for what may happen, and their collective decisions bring the new moment into being.

If the future does not exist, then you and I, the grass, the birds, the earth, the moon, sun and stars, even space itself—the entire universe—must be bursting into existence in each moment. What kind of a world can do this? It cannot be a world composed of hard, unchanging substances that endure unchanged under all the surface appearances of change. This must be a world in which energy erupts anew in each moment. Is this true?

Just look at your own experience. Isn't that exactly what your own experience is like? New drops of experience pop into being one after another like "buds or drops of perception" (*PR* 68, quoting William James). Each new drop of awareness is incredibly complex, composed of thoughts, feelings, sensory experiences, and deeper feelings of being surrounded by a world of causal forces. You can never make thoughts stand still.

Your own flow of experience is a paradigm for the process-relational vision of reality laid out in Whitehead's work and in the book you are currently reading. We will keep coming back to this paradigm to see it from different angles and to see its complexity.

PROCESS AND RELATEDNESS

The interwoven, relational character of our world and our lives is glaringly obvious to thoughtful people today. The World Wide Web of the Internet impacts everyone who reads this book—even if they never go online. People commonly exchange email with others around the globe. Globalization is simply a name for the fact that our world economy is so interrelated that jobs can move anywhere in the world, restructuring the entire global economy. Human activities appear to be changing the world climate, creating global warming, and causing massive extinctions of animal species.

Equally glaring is the fact that these relationships are dynamic processes. Our world of rock stars, political borders, computers, and medical technology changes so fast that no one can keep up. Never has it been clearer, as Heraclitus observed twenty-five hundred years ago, that you can't step in the same river twice. Indeed, as his student Cratylus argued, you can't even step in the same river once. The river changes even as we step into it, and so do we. Some things change very slowly, but all things change. Or, to put it better, the world is not finally made of "things" at all, if a "thing" is something that exists over time without changing. The world is composed of events and processes.

Process philosophers claim that these features of relatedness and process are not mere surface appearance: They go all the way down to the roots of reality. Moreover, process thinkers insist that our failure to recognize that reality is a relational process is a source of great harms. It matters how we think about reality, the world, and ourselves because we act on what we think.

One function of philosophy is to help us see obvious truths more clearly and deeply. Another function is to challenge ideas that appear obvious but that may be fundamentally mistaken. Process philosophy is an effort to think clearly and deeply about the obvious truth that our world and our lives are dynamic, interrelated processes and to challenge the apparently obvious, but fundamentally mistaken, idea that the world (including ourselves) is made of *things* that exist independently of such relationships and that seem to endure unchanged through all the processes of change.

Philosophers have struggled for millennia over how best to think about our experiences of both permanence and change—about the relationship between Being and Becoming. By and large, unchanging Being has taken priority in Western philosophy and religion, while Becoming often has primacy in Asian culture, although there are important exceptions in both cases. In the West, Plato firmly established the primacy of Being when he argued that this world of change is merely a shadowy copy of a realm of eternally unchanging forms. Following the Platonists (not the Bible), Western Christian theologians asserted that God was the ultimate unchanging reality. Finally, in the Enlightenment, René Descartes and others argued for Being over Becoming by insisting (contrary to many of their own observations) that the world is composed of physical and mental "substances," especially including human souls, that (1) exist independently and (2) endure unchanged through change. Thus, Descartes imported Platonic and heavenly immutability into this world of objects and human minds. Our own minds (or souls) are, for Cartesian thinkers, primary instances of *things* that are *not* relational and *not* dynamic processes. Cartesian dualism, like many philosophies before it, became baptized into the Christian faith and powerfully shaped the Christian view of the self in the West.

This nonrelational character of Cartesian dualism, especially as combined with Christian theology, was intensified by the belief that this immaterial mental substance could not possibly arise out of nature. Since early modern philosophers and scientists envisioned the world as made out of nonexperiencing matter, it seemed clear that no natural (that is, material) process could possibly give rise to human minds/souls. The only alternative, they thought, was to assume that souls were created supernaturally by divine fiat. Consequently, human minds came to be seen as essentially unrelated to the world of nature around us.

Process philosophers, on the other hand, argue that there is urgency in coming to see the world as a web of interrelated processes of which we are integral parts, so that all of our choices and actions have consequences for the world around us. This stance requires us to challenge and reject the prevailing philosophies and theologies that give primacy to Being over Becoming, to independence over relatedness, to things over processes, to the idea that the human spirit is fundamentally isolated from the social and natural web in which we clearly all live and move and are becoming.

Yes, of course, there is something important about the ideas of permanence, of Being, and of standing as our own independent person regardless of what anyone else says. But what is important here is better understood and more wisely addressed by rooting even the endurance of things in the deeper recognition that nothing stays the same forever and that no person is an island. Or, as someone suggested, people are islands, but islands aren't what they appear to be. Deeper down, even islands, like waves, are merely faces of a deeper unity. If we cannot see that unity, we imperil the web in which we live.

Process thinkers, along with modern physicists, emphasize that relatedness and process go all the way down and all the way up. Process theologians, such as John B. Cobb Jr., Marjorie Suchocki, and David Ray Griffin, argue that even God is best understood in terms of relatedness and process rather than as an unchanging, static Being unaffected by the world. It will be my task in this book to articulate as briefly and clearly as I can a process-relational vision of reality, arguments for that vision, and the important implications it has for understanding every aspect of our lives.

SO WHAT?

Learning to value diversity is one of the vital tasks we face if we are to live together in our modern world. Travel and communication bring together people from a world of different cultural, religious, spiritual, intellectual, and scientific perspectives. This diversity can be a rich source of inspiration, yet we also need to find visions that can speak effectively to as many of these different communities as possible. We need shared visions that can help integrate religion with science and ancient worldviews with more modern ones and that can help us learn how to value diversity as it helps integrate diverse perspectives.

Process-relational thought has enormous potential for integrating and unifying the richly different perspectives of people in the world today. Of course, the community of process thinkers includes people with important differences of thought. What good would an intellectual vision be if it didn't inspire creative challenge within a community? But it also brings people from very different backgrounds into that conversation. Our world is very much in need of an intellectual, scientific, and spiritual vision that can draw many different people into a unified conversation, while still stimulating further exploration and challenge.

LOOKING AHEAD

How do we go about constructing and evaluating a vision of the whole of reality? That question will be the focus of the next chapter.

Imaginative Generalization 2

THE SEARCH FOR A COMPREHENSIVE VISION

Rationalism never shakes off its status as an experimental adventure.
—Alfred North Whitehead, *Process and Reality*

Everything is tied together. That is a fundamental premise as basic to modern physics and biology as to ancient Hinduism and Buddhism. While degrees of influence vary, you and I are in this world together, along with every dolphin, whale, rat, bat, ant, bee, amoeba, and electron. Our growing awareness of ourselves as inescapably woven into the ecological web of life and of our power to damage that delicate web demands that we stop thinking of ourselves and the world in terms of isolated atoms and "self-made men" and begin thinking in terms of relationships and processes. If reality is interconnected, relational, and dynamic, then thinking solely in terms of separation and changeless being is dangerous. Our ability to make sense of the world is at stake. The quality of our lives is at stake. Indeed, our survival is at stake. I don't mean that our survival as a species depends on everyone becoming a process-relational philosopher, but I do mean that unless we can take seriously the ecological, cultural, religious, and economic interwovenness of our lives in this world, we are in serious danger of self-destruction. Process philosophy can help us come to that vital self-understanding.

Philosophy is born of wonder; it is the art of wondering in a disciplined, thoughtful way. What is everything, anyway? Are we really free? How are our minds and bodies related? Do animals have souls like ours? How can I know any of this?

Modern sciences are also born of wonder, sharpened by the need to solve concrete problems and by the success of specific methods. The success of science has led many people, including many philosophers, to see speculative philosophy (metaphysics) as a waste of time we would do better to avoid. The task of philosophy, many have argued, should primarily be the clarification of language.

Alfred North Whitehead shared this concern about the metaphysical philosophies of his time. In the early modern period, from the seventeenth through the nineteenth centuries, metaphysics and science were one project—"natural philosophy"—the effort to create a new and useful vision of the nature of our world. Whitehead argued, however, that by the end of the nineteenth century, philosophy had fallen so far behind science that it was unable to help scientists in their thinking. Rather than reject the metaphysical challenge, he set out to create a new vision that incorporated the best science of his day and that could actually be of use to scientists and others.

BOLD HUMILITY

Whitehead saw speculative philosophy (metaphysics) *not* as talk about a transcendental realm beyond all possible human knowledge but as an effort to generalize our knowledge, to seek a way of understanding the world as comprehensively as we can. In that respect, you might think of it as parallel to Einstein's search for a grand unified theory. Can we conceive a view of the world that will, in principle, connect all of our experience and knowledge into a single, unified system of thought? Such an effort would face the challenge of bringing together the physical sciences with the social sciences and even with aesthetics, morality, and religion (*PR* xii). This is surely a daunting task, but Whitehead felt it was important to try. Perhaps what I like best about Whitehead is that he undertook this magnificently bold quest with an attitude of tremendous humility.

The boldness of Whitehead's quest is obvious—a theory of absolutely everything that is or ever could be.

> At the end, in so far as the enterprise has been successful, there should be no problem of space-time, or of epistemology, or of causality, left over for discussion. The scheme

> should have developed all of those generic notions adequate for the expression of any possible interconnection of things. (*PR* xii)

There is nothing half-hearted about this goal. Whitehead isn't just wondering about how everything that *exists* is connected but about how everything that could *possibly* exist is connected. That is a *very* bold quest.

Yet, Whitehead's boldness was far from arrogance or dogmatism. He was very keenly aware of Plato's remark in the *Timaeus* that the best we could hope for was "a likely tale." So, at the very outset Whitehead reminds us that

> There remains the final reflection, how shallow, puny, and imperfect are efforts to sound the depths in the nature of things. In philosophical discussion, the merest hint of dogmatic certainty as to finality of statement is an exhibition of folly. (*PR* xiv)

Anyone who has read the *Apology* of Socrates should understand the imperative that we must not pretend to know what we do not know. The loss of such intellectual humility marks the beginning of a closed mind and a closed system of thought. "Speculative boldness must be balanced by complete humility before logic, and before fact" (*PR* 17). Yet, humility without boldness of thought can be laziness, an excuse for caving in to the cynical argument of the Sophists that we cannot know anything so there is no reason to inquire. It is possible to have new insights, broader insights, that can help us both to solve old problems and to see new problems waiting round the corner.

SPECULATIVE PHILOSOPHY AS IMAGINATIVE GENERALIZATION

Whitehead's philosophy appeals to both reason and experience. Neither alone is sufficient to deal with life in this world.

> Speculative philosophy is the endeavour to frame a coherent, logical, necessary system of general ideas in terms of

> which every element of our experience can be interpreted. By this notion of "interpretation" I mean that everything of which we are conscious, as enjoyed, perceived, willed, or thought shall have the character of a particular instance of the general scheme. Thus the philosophical scheme should be coherent, logical, and in respect to its interpretation, applicable and adequate. Here "applicable" means that some items of experience are thus interpretable, and "adequate" means that there are no items incapable of such interpretation. (*PR* 3)

Our ideas about the world should hang together. That is what it means for them to be *coherent*. This thought would seem obvious enough to any beginning philosopher, but achieving the goal isn't easy to do. Time and again great thinkers have gotten to a sticking point in their own efforts where they just couldn't get the puzzle pieces to fit together. So, as Whitehead observed, they just left pieces out. For example, David Hume, an eighteenth-century philosopher who was a wonderfully honest and bold thinker, frankly admitted that he could not find any way for us actually to know that causation happened. All we can *see* is the sequence of events, not causation. So, Hume admitted that he believed in causation but could not make it fit in his theory of knowledge. In the same way René Descartes honestly acknowledged that he experienced a "union" or "co-mingling" of body and mind, but that unity did not fit into his system of thought, so he simply took that piece out and declared mind and body to be totally distinct kinds of reality. Those are just two key examples of the failures of coherence that Whitehead wanted to avoid.

It seems equally obvious that any effort to create a comprehensive description of the world should be *logical*. But time and again, especially in religious thought, people get to a problem their system cannot solve (like why a perfectly good and powerful God allows so much evil in the world) and simply say that God's logic is not ours, so our theology doesn't have to be logical or that our moral standards just don't apply to God. They claim we can just rely on faith and mystery. There is certainly plenty of mystery in the world if by *mystery* we mean things we don't understand and may never understand. Also, it is true that many elements of the world, like human emotions, are not themselves logical. That is very different from saying that *our ideas* about those things can simply be illogical—self-contradictory. They are, after all, *our ideas*, and our ideas *are* governed by the rules of logic or else they are useless, even if they are ideas about God.

It is not enough, however, for our ideas to be rational—coherent and logical; they must be *applicable*. In other words, to be of value they must tell us about the world we experience and live in. They must tell us about *something in particular*, not just everything in general. So far as ideas explain particular situations, they can be said to be applicable. Applicability seems as obvious as the criteria of being coherent and logical. But it is precisely the failure to apply to anything concrete that has made so many metaphysical systems seem foolish and worthless. Philosophy that isn't applicable to anything is what leads people to make fun of "mere metaphysics" and to dismiss it as illogical nonsense. Whitehead insists that his system must avoid this intellectual sin. It is also why he tends to speak less of metaphysics and more of speculative philosophy, or imaginative and descriptive generalization.

The boldness of Whitehead's vision, of course, moves beyond being applicable and strives to create a system of ideas that will be *adequate*. Adequate to what? Everything. This is the really hard part. Can we possibly form a scheme of ideas that will include the most basic principles of reality that apply to everything that ever is or ever could be? We can try. Adequacy is a matter of degree, but those degrees matter. We are faced with a vast, complex world in which we encounter a wide range of *interconnected* problems. The better our ideas are at helping us to see how the world and those problems are interconnected, the more successfully we can work to solve our problems.

> Rationalism never shakes off its status of an experimental adventure. . . . Rationalism is an adventure in the clarification of thought, progressive and never final. But it is an adventure in which even partial success has importance. (*PR* 9)

So, if we are going to create this coherent and logical system of ideas that is not only applicable to something in particular but struggles as far as it can toward adequacy—toward describing the basic principles that apply to everything that is or possibly could be—how do we go about it? What method does Whitehead propose?

First, let me explain what Whitehead doesn't do. You may recall René Descartes' search for that one idea, that one truth that was absolutely certain beyond all possibility of doubt. If you were to look at the works of early modern philosophers like Descartes, Benedictus de Spinoza, or Gottfried Wilhelm Leibniz, you would easily see how much they hungered for the certainty achieved by mathematics. They modeled their systems on mathematics, beginning with definitions and axioms and building on them as if they were perfectly clear, self-evident principles beyond all possible doubt. They hoped that if, like mathematics, they started with absolutely certain truths and carefully checked each step of the argument, they could build a whole system of knowledge that would itself be certain.

Despite the very understandable attraction of the mathematical model, Whitehead, himself a great mathematician, thought these philosophers had made a serious mistake in adopting it. "Philosophy has been haunted by the unfortunate notion that its method is dogmatically to indicate premises which are severally clear, distinct, and certain; and to erect upon those premises a deductive system of thought" (*PR* 8) . The deepest aspect of this mistake is that "metaphysical categories are not dogmatic statements of the obvious; they are tentative formulations of the ultimate generalities" (*PR* 8). Here again the element of humility emerges in Whitehead's thinking. It just won't do to begin our system, or to end it, with such claims to certainty.

Consequently, Whitehead took a different path.

> The true method of discovery is like the flight of an aeroplane. It starts from the ground of particular observation; it makes a flight in the thin air of imaginative generalization; and it again lands for renewed observation rendered acute by rational interpretation. (*PR* 5)

Think of the method this way. Start with a very basic principle underlying (*applicable* to) one specific discipline like physics. Tinker with it a bit, and *imagine* what it would be like if that properly broadened principle also applied to some other field of thought like biology. Be careful that you don't cheat by just equivocating on the meanings of your words. Then go and look. See if the expanded principle really can be made to generalize across both fields.[1] If the observed facts and careful reasoning support your effort, you have made a step toward the larger general principles of thought. Your revised principle is now more *adequate* than it was before and it can stand as a *descriptive generalization*. But, of course, this task becomes more and more difficult as the principles apply to more and more fields. When you get around to those principles that describe the basic features of any existing thing at all, the task requires a combination of creative, imaginative, and disciplined thought that few people possess.

EXPERIENCE AND THE LIMITS OF LANGUAGE

Finally, we return to the theme of boldness and humility. Whitehead believed that "[t]here is no first principle which is in itself unknowable, not to be captured by a flash of insight" (*PR* 4). Important insights are possible to get to the root of an idea, to its "first principle." Yet, that conviction is different from claiming that we can successfully capture a comprehensive system of such principles. Whitehead pointed to some reasons for the inevitable tentativeness and partialness of our success. He especially noted the problem of language: "Words and phrases must be stretched towards a generality foreign to their ordinary usage; and however such elements of language be stabilized as technicalities, they remain metaphors mutely appealing for an imaginative leap" (*PR* 4).

The problem of language is one reason that it is so difficult to read Whitehead. He was trying to express a new vision that fundamentally challenged many "common-sense" ideas.[2] After all, "[i]n some measure or other, progress is always a transcendence of the obvious" (*PR* 9). For better or worse, our common sense (our inherited set of beliefs) about the "obvious" is expressed in our ordinary language. Ideas that challenge and transcend those traditions cannot simply be expressed in the common language. We must either redefine old words—generating confusion because we keep thinking of their older meanings—or create new ones—generating confusion because they are so foreign. In either case, it does no good to complain, "Why can't he just say what he means?" What he means cannot simply be expressed in the familiar language.

SO WHAT?

Whitehead suggested that morality is tied up with breadth of vision. If I see my life as totally disconnected from others, no moral vision is possible. It is only as I see that you and I are connected, that our lives and actions affect each other, that the possibility of ethical thought and action emerges. How often, though, do we struggle to communicate even the simplest aspects of our connectedness to each other? Words and actions can have meanings we never imagined. We teachers have learned that we might offer a friendly and supportive hug to a student, unaware that they have previously been abused by a teacher. Even on daily matters miscommunication is common. My wife and I have been married nearly thirty-seven years, and when we still stumble over simple failures of communications we joke, "Maybe when we've know each other longer."

Imagine, then, the challenges faced by the authors of the Hindu Upanishads and the Bhagavad-Gita as they struggled to communicate a vision of ultimate reality. When Krishna sought to explain himself as a manifestation of this ultimate reality to Arjuna, imagine the authors of this passage seeking adequate language.

> I am the Atman that dwells in the heart of every mortal creature:
> I am the beginning, the life-span, and the end of all. . . .
> I am the sacred syllable OM: . . .
> . . . among those who measure, I am Time: . . .
> I am death that snatches all: I, also, am the source of all
> that shall be born: . . .
> I am the dice-play of the cunning: . . .
> I am the knowledge of the knower. . . .
> Know only that I exist, and that one atom of myself sustains
> the universe.[3]

LOOKING AHEAD

One key example of the struggle that we will face over and over again is the word *experience*. In this case Whitehead chose to keep an old word and make it do new things. But to make it do those new things, it has to be one of those words that get "stretched towards a generality foreign to their ordinary usage" (*PR* 4). You will see that stretching done in the following chapters. My strategy is to ask you to begin with your own experience (so that the ideas are sure to be applicable) and then stretch your usual thinking about "experience" so far that it takes you places you have never been before, but that you will recognize when you get there because it will be a better description of your experience and the world than you've had before. "The ultimate test is always widespread, recurrent experience; and the more general the rationalistic scheme, the more important is this final appeal" (*PR* 17).

Minds, Bodies, and Experience 3

ENVISIONING A UNIFIED SELF

It is said that "men are rational." This is palpably false: they are only intermittently rational—merely liable to rationality.

—ALFRED NORTH WHITEHEAD, *PROCESS AND REALITY*

LET'S START with you. What is it like to be you? What is it like to be an experiencing person in the world? You will be my touchstone of applicability. I'm going to appeal to your own experience of yourself to explain Whitehead's philosophy and to show what difference it makes. The goal, of course, will be to extend these insights outward toward everything that is.

YOU ARE PART OF THE WORLD

You, after all, are part of everything that exists. As distinctively wonderful as you are, you are not totally unique or isolated from all the rest. You are an example of how the whole world is because you are part of the world, interwoven with everything that is, a thread in the fabric of the same system of natural laws and interconnecting causes as everything else.

There is a Hindu and Buddhist metaphor that the self is a drop of water and that the goal of life is to return to the cosmic ocean where individuality is lost in the whole. Actually, Hindus and Buddhists would say that we are already part of that ocean, but we are trapped in an illusion of separateness. The world of things is only a mask that conceals the unity of the whole. Process philosophers would agree that we are like a drop of water in the ocean of reality in the sense of affirming that we are fully a part of that larger whole, like a drop of water is part of the ocean. Whatever composes the world composes us, too.

Yet, Whitehead would not have seen the diversity of the world as an illusion to be escaped but simply as something to be understood and appreciated. The same point is made by the contemporary Buddhist Thich Nhat Hanh when he advises:

> Don't get caught in theories or ideas, such as saying that suffering is an illusion or that we have to "transcend" both suffering and joy. Just stay in touch with what is actually going on, and you will touch the true nature of suffering and the true nature of joy. When you have a headache, it would not be correct to call your headache illusory. To help it go away, you have to acknowledge its existence and understand its causes.[1]

Whitehead made somewhat the same point when he observed wryly that "[t]here are simplicities connected with the motion of a bar of steel which are obscured if we refuse to abstract from the individual molecules" (*PR* 16). The task is to understand better the relationship between individuality and interconnectedness, between the one and the many. Although Buddhist and Hindu thinkers may rightly give priority to the ultimacy of oneness for some purposes, when I wish to keep my child from running in front of a truck, it is more useful to work in the realm of the many. Descartes argued correctly that the *fact* that you are experiencing cannot itself be an illusion, even if the particular contents of an experience or the concepts that frame it might be. So it is true both that your individuality is one of the touchstones of reality and that all of reality is a single woven whole.

STRANGERS IN A STRANGE LAND?

The idea that we are fully interwoven with the natural world may seem obvious to modern readers who are aware of evolution and ecology, yet there has been, and still is, a powerful side of the Western tradition, strengthened by Christian theology and many philosophers of the seventeenth and eighteenth centuries, insisting that we are *not* part of this world. It is common to think of God as having first created the physical world with one set of principles and rules—natural law—and then creating us with a supernatural soul that is in this world but not of it, making us strangers in a strange land. We are just too wonderful, it is said, for us to be part of the muck and mire of the rest of the world.

Plato had suggested that the human soul is part of the eternal realm of unchangeable reality, distinct from the physical world (including the human body) that becomes and perishes and "never really is."[2] Christians (influenced by Plato) have often argued that the physical world (including our own bodies) exists only to serve God's purpose of saving (or damning) human souls and that the world as we know it will pass away, while our eternal souls remain. In the view of early modern natural philosophers like Descartes, Francis Bacon, and Isaac Newton, everything else in the world but the human soul is composed of atoms (like tiny billiard balls) moving in a void, totally determined by natural law, while the human soul is supernatural and free of those laws. Thus, what looks to us as a thoroughly secular science was originally part of an effort to separate human souls from the natural world in order to provide support for traditional Christian belief in the supernatural nature and immortality of the soul.[3]

In that world of early modern science, human beings were sometimes seen as the only ones in this world having any experience at all. Yes, God and angels and devils had experience, too; but in the world of nature, nothing had experience because the physical world was built of atoms that were simply very tiny pieces of matter that were lifeless and totally devoid of experience. Hence, nothing made of them could have any experience either. Since our own bodies were believed to be composed of such atoms, there was no way to explain how even *our* bodies could have any experience. It was only *super*natural, divinely created human souls that could have experience in this otherwise mechanical, barren, atoms-in-the-void, nonexperiencing natural world. Human souls, they believed, are *not* part of the natural world.

There is one other important reason why people have insisted on a dualism of minds and bodies. Descartes claimed to have proved the

Christian doctrine of the immortality of the soul. If the soul exists separately from the body and has a supernatural origin, then it need not die with the body. Most people fear death, so the desire that we and our loved ones should live forever makes a dualistic worldview attractive, whether or not it is true.

A NOTE ON LANGUAGE

Let me pause for a brief note on language. How shall we speak of the experiencing self? The term *mind* often suggests our rational side, while *soul* is often restricted to a religious context and commonly emphasizes belief in a supernatural self. *Self* may focus too much on our sense of identity. John Cobb Jr. suggests that perhaps the term *psyche* is useful since it carries less baggage, precisely because it is less commonly used. So we face the same problems Whitehead so often confronted. A similar problem exists with terms like *experience*, *feeling*, *thinking*, or *conceptual*.

Because this is a beginning introduction, I will stick to more familiar language like *mind*, *self*, and *soul*, and will work hard to remind you to think of these words in new ways. Whitehead placed great emphasis on emotion. For that reason, I will often speak of experience and feeling because they are general by definition and because they tend not to focus attention on our rational dimensions. We usually speak of feeling both physical sensations and emotions and almost never speak of feeling ourselves reasoning.

So you will find me arguing that the mind/soul/self/psyche is the flow of the body's experience or feeling. Sometimes that self includes a flow of reasoning, but it takes little attention to see how much more deeply our physical/emotional feelings run than do our fleeting moments of reasoning. Since we will be focusing on what we share in common with other experiencers in this world, the flow of felt emotion will emerge as the great ocean on which the thin layer of rationality precariously floats. As Whitehead observed, "It is said that 'men are rational.' This is palpably false: they are only intermittently rational—merely liable to rationality. . . . The intellect of Socrates is intermittent: he occasionally sleeps and he can be drugged or stunned" (*PR* 79).

WE ARE EXAMPLES, NOT EXCEPTIONS

Especially since Charles Darwin, it has become increasingly clear that we *are* part of the natural world, that we are completely interwoven with everything. We are unique in some ways, but not in others, and our uniqueness is a matter of degree rather than of kind. We are part of the same causal web of interconnections as everything else that exists. Many of us now find this view of ourselves and of the world beyond dispute, but that does not mean that we fully understand what it means or how it works. Understanding how you and I fit within the larger world of nature and causality was one of the central tasks Whitehead undertook.

One helpful consequence of the view that we are part of the world rather than separate from it is that, by looking at our own existence, we can learn something about the rules that apply to everything that exists. We are examples of those rules, not exceptions to them. The world is like us because we are like the world, part of the world, reflecting the same basic principles and rules as the world. We cannot understand ourselves without understanding the world of which we are a part; nor can we finally understand the world without understanding ourselves as part of it. Yes, we must beware of anthropomorphism, of simply making animals, God, and the world look like us in a self-centered way. But it is the reverse of anthropomorphism to acknowledge that we are simply instances of how everything else in the universe works, that we are not supernatural exceptions. As Whitehead observed:

> It is the accepted doctrine in physical science that a living body is to be interpreted according to what is known of other sections of the physical universe. This is a sound axiom; but it is double-edged. For it carries with it the converse deduction that other sections of the universe are to be interpreted in accordance with what we know of the human body (*PR* 119).

Let us follow Whitehead's method of an airplane, beginning from this ground of fact, and take off into the air of imagination. What if human minds are not the only ones to have experience?

DOES YOUR BODY EXPERIENCE?

First, let's think about whether your *body* experiences.

Briefly, consider why people might not think so. Probably you don't think that this book or the desk or chair or other physical objects around you have experience. Since they are physical and your body is physical, perhaps your body does not experience either. Perhaps it *is* only your mind that has experience.

That, of course, was René Descartes' main line of thought. Descartes was a dualist. He believed that the universe is made of two kinds of substances—mental substances and physical substances—and that the two are radically different and separate. He saw minds as purely thinking things that had two properties: They think, and they do not exist in space. He saw all physical bodies as having two opposing properties: They do not think, and they exist in space. Since he also included hunger and thirst as "confused modes of thought," we will be justified, I think, in expanding his language a little to say that minds experience, while bodies do not.

Is that what it is really like to be you? Do you really live as a purely intellectual, purely rational mind within a body that has no experience at all?

There are some obvious problems with this sharp division between minds and bodies. Lift a hand, wiggle a toe, or just blink your eyes. How did you do that? Your mind made your body do it, we assume. But if Descartes were right, it would be impossible. Your mind is not in space, so it could not push on your brain or nerves to move your hand, toe, or eyelid. Nor could your mind send your body a thought, like "Move your toe."[4] According to Descartes, your body cannot think, so it cannot receive any thoughts or feelings from your mind. Similarly, your body cannot send any experiences to your mind because the body has no experience to send. Nor can it push on the mind because the mind is not in space. Cartesian dualism makes the most obvious events of our embodied existence impossible.

Touch something and *feel* the sensation on your skin. Rap your knuckles sharply on a desk and *feel* the pain in your knuckles. Taste something spicy and *feel* the tingle on your tongue and lips. (If it is appropriate and convenient, kiss or hug someone and *feel* those pressures on your lips or arms.) Wait until you are hungry and feel the hunger in your stomach. What is it like to be you? Does your body have experience?

Of course, we know that without our brains we would not be able to have conscious experiences of such feelings. We also know that people who have lost arms or legs can feel phantom pain in those limbs. Yet the role of the brain in our feelings, including phantom feelings, is itself a proof that the body *is* experiencing, for the brain is part of the body, and if the brain is damaged in certain ways, we stop feeling consciously.

Come back to your bodily feelings. We sometimes have the clearly mistaken idea that our mind is like a little Cartesian person in a room inside our heads. (There are some wonderful *Calvin and Hobbes* cartoons where the little Calvin inside his head pulls levers and turns knobs to control the big Calvin body.) But we know this is not how it works.

We experience *with* our bodies. Our eyes are not holes through which a little person inside looks to see outside. If eyes were just holes, the little person would be able to see better if our eyes were removed and the holes enlarged. No, we see *with* our eyes, not through them. Remove our eyes and we cannot see. In the same way, our ears are not holes for that little person to listen at. If our ears were just holes, then removing our ears and making the holes larger would improve our hearing. Rather, we hear *with* our eardrums.

The same is true of all our sense organs. We smell *with* our nose, taste *with* our tongues, feel *with* our skin. In every case, we also feel *with* our nervous system and our brain. Remove any vital part and we stop having that experience. (See *PR* 62–64 and elsewhere.)

It is true that if you lose an arm or a leg you can still think. That is simply because thinking and remembering, etc., are done with the brain rather than with your arms or legs. Still, an important source of experience has been lost with the missing limb. You can no longer reach out with your hand and have the experiences arising from touching things or burning your fingers. Phantom experiences don't really come from the missing limbs. You may have experiences that seem to come from those limbs, but they are products of disrupted nerve endings and the brain. You have lost the power to experience *with* that arm or leg.

By the same token, if you damage a portion of your brain by injury, drugs, disease, or a stroke, you may damage or destroy the ability to think, feel, remember, or imagine with that part of your brain. Because we think *with* our brain, just as we see *with* our eyes, a perfectly conscious person with an undamaged brain can be trapped "inside" a body that is blind and deaf.[5] But a fully conscious person cannot exist "inside" a brain if the portions of the brain that make that consciousness possible are destroyed. We experience *with* our bodies—including our brains—which means that our bodies experience.

The very power of our bodily experience sometimes provides great psychological urgency for people to deny the connection. Sufficiently terrible physical and emotional trauma can powerfully motivate us to preserve our sense of self by disengaging from our body. The point is made clearly in a Tarzan movie when Jane appears on the verge of being gang raped, and her father cries out, "Remember, you are not your body." This reassurance makes great sense in that context, as it must make sense for many real people in real tragedies. If your body is about to be assaulted and humiliated, it makes powerful emotional sense to separate your sense of self from those bodily traumas. In extreme cases, we know that people sometimes dissociate from their bodies, so that they literally have no conscious memory afterward of what happened to them. Similarly, those whose physical condition is severely limiting in some way, for example, if they are quadriplegic, will understandably focus their sense of self on their mental and emotional experiences and abilities.

However powerful and understandable these psychological motives are for separating our sense of self from our bodily life, we can recognize the tragedy inherent in a life so painful that people must cut themselves off from so much of their own deepest experiences. It is precisely the power and depth of those experiences, or lost experiences, that motivate the effort at separation. But we cannot fully separate ourselves from what we are—living, experiencing bodies.

Even René Descartes admitted the impossibility of dualism at some moments in his meditations. He was honest enough to acknowledge, counter to his own philosophy, that our minds are "mingled" with our bodies and "united" with them.

> By means of these feelings of pain, hunger, thirst and so on, nature also teaches me that I am present to my body not merely in the way a seaman is present to his ship, but that I am tightly joined and, so to speak, mingled together with it. For otherwise, when the body is wounded, I, who am nothing but a thing that thinks, would not then sense the pain. Rather, I would perceive the wound by means of the pure intellect, just as a seaman perceives by means of sight whether anything in the ship is broken. When the body lacks food or drink, I would understand this in a clear-cut fashion; I would not have confused feelings of hunger and thirst. For certainly these feelings of thirst, hunger, pain, and so on are nothing but confused modes of thinking arising from the union and, as it were, the mingling of the mind and body.[6]

But these clear facts did not fit Descartes' larger purposes, so he simply set them aside—a major example of the incoherence in first principles that Whitehead sought to overcome. When Princess Elisabeth wrote to him making these points and arguing that his radical dualism simply could not explain what we all know to be true, Descartes finally conceded and suggested (ironically, I have to say) that belief in the dualism of mind and body was the result of excessive meditation:

> Hence it follows that those who never philosophize and who use only their senses do not doubt that the soul moves the body and that the body acts on the soul. But they consider the two as a single thing, that is, they consider the union of the two and to consider the union between two things is to consider them as one single thing. . . . [I]t is by means of ordinary life and conversations and in abstaining from meditation and from studying things which exercise the imagination, that one learns to conceive the union of soul and body.[7]

SO WHAT?

Affirming ourselves as fully embodied creatures can have powerful consequences. Let me offer only one kind of example. All too often, the insistence that our souls are supernatural—hence, not of this world and not even of this body—has had terrible consequences in religion. If we are really strangers in this world, then it does not matter very much what happens to our bodies or even what happens in this world.

To illustrate this, I turn to Manlio Argueta's powerful novel *One Day of Life*. Argueta shows us the world through the eyes of Lupe, a peasant woman suffering brutal oppression by government forces during the peasant revolution in El Salvador. Lupe describes the religion that served the interests of the powerful landowners.

> Once upon a time the priests would come and hold Mass in the Detour's chapel, giving us hope: "Hang on just a little longer." They'd tell us not to worry, that heaven was ours, that on earth we should live humbly but that in the kingdom of heaven we would be happy. That we shouldn't care about worldly things. And when we'd tell the priests that our children were dying from worms, they'd recommend resignation.... The priests would tell us to be patient. ... Well, what is there to do? May God's will be done.

Then, Lupe tells us, there came new priests (reflecting the attitudes of Vatican II):

> They started getting us into cooperatives. To help each other, to share profits. It's wonderful to help someone, to live in peace with everyone. ... What's important is that our children don't die. To let a child die is the worst sin one can commit."[8]

The contrast between such views of human life motivated Robert McAfee Brown, a theologian deeply involved in Latin American struggles of liberation, to assert a new working principle for his own life as a theologian. From now on, he said, "[A]ny future theology I do must put the welfare of children above the niceties of metaphysics.

Any theology that provides for the creative growth of children will make it satisfactorily on all other scores."[9]

A working principle like this demands that we take seriously the embodiment of children and of all living creatures. Hunger, abuse, disease, and poverty matter to our whole being, not just to a body to which we are accidentally attached. We should be reminded that, in the Hebrew Bible, which also affirmed that people are fully embodied persons, there was a powerful sense of social justice, a deep recognition that the physical condition of persons matters at every level.

While process-relational philosophy does not commit one to a single position on ethical issues of the day, it certainly has a profound impact on the way we think about them. Consider, for example, the important consequences for the current American debate over abortion that so many people think of the human soul as a supernatural entity—totally undetectable by modern science—that is implanted by God at the moment of conception. Consider what difference it would make if we think of the mind or soul as the cumulative flow of the body's experience and seek to study the point at which a human body (especially a human brain) is capable of producing that unique flow of experience that then interacts with the body and functions as its mind. There is still an important discussion to be engaged, but it will be shaped differently in such a philosophical framework.

Acknowledging our full embodiment does not mean denying all of the wonderful range of experiences that we usually think of as spiritual. Rather, it means broadening our vision of the spiritual to include the physical and to see value where we have not seen it before. But that, perhaps, can be seen more clearly in future chapters.

LOOKING AHEAD

What is it like to be you? I experience with my body. Do you? Recognizing that you may need to think further about this, let us consider for now that you, too, experience *with* your body, which means that your body has experience. If that is so, then at least one part of the physical world has experience. If that part of the physical world can experience, contrary to Descartes' dualistic categories, just how far down does experience go? That is the question for our next flight.

4 Experience All the Way Down

SEEKING AN IMAGINATIVE LEAP

Words and phrases must be stretched towards a generality foreign to their ordinary usage; and however such elements of language be stabilized as technicalities, they remain metaphors mutely appealing for an imaginative leap.

—Alfred North Whitehead, *Process and Reality*

What does it mean to believe that our bodies are capable of experiencing, that your mind is only the central hub of a wealth of experience arising from the cells of your body? Using Whitehead's airplane metaphor, let us consider what it might be like if this principle extends beyond our own bodies. If experience is not limited to human minds but is also present in the physical world, how far does it go? Does experience go all the way down to the most basic, most simple, most fundamental building blocks of the world?

EXPERIENCE IN OTHER ANIMALS

What if dogs have experience, too? Many people would take this to be as obvious as the claim that other people have experience. It has often been argued, however, that nonhuman animals have no experience and that believing that they do is a naive act of anthropomorphism, of projecting our own feelings onto them. It is true, of course, that we must be wary of anthropomorphism. Surely all of us play at personalizing animals and even cars, teddy bears, and other objects in ways we know are fanciful, but I have not yet met a dog owner who believed for a minute that their dog had *no* experience.

Since I don't know about your relationship to nonhuman animals, let me tell you about some of my own dogs over the years. My dogs act for all the world as if they experience happiness, pain, pleasure, fear, affection, anger, and worry. I see no evidence that they do math or philosophy, but their sense of guilt seems to be very much like rudimentary human guilt—the internalized anticipation of external punishments. Our own earliest and most basic feelings of guilt are probably just anticipations of punishment, which are gradually internalized. Similarly, when my dogs had been scolded often enough for peeing on the carpet, they learned to feel bad about it (anticipate punishment for it) even before I found the wet spot. When I walked in the door after such an incident, they dropped their ears and tails and looked just as they did when, in the past, I had caught them in the act and scolded them. So, given the signs, I went looking for the wet spot or whatever it is they did.[1] Although we humans weave these feelings with our moral reasoning into a much larger awareness of moral context, the starting points seem the same in us as in my dogs.

Perhaps even more revealing is the fact that my dogs have uniformly shown an ability to envision a possible future that they take action to bring about. They pick up a ball and come to where I am, perhaps resting their head in my lap until I throw the ball. If I am too stupid to catch on, they may drop the ball and then catch it to show me what they want. Rachel, the beagle, would finally drop the ball down the basement stairs and run down and retrieve it until I caught on. My golden retrievers would frequently get their leash and bring it to me. When I finally stood up and acted as if I understood their intention—perhaps by saying the word *walk* or just by picking up my shoes—they would jump up and down and run to the door, perhaps rewarding me for my intelligent response.

Currently we have two young golden retrievers. Ellie, the smaller one, learned to nudge the door knob with her nose when she needed to go out. Then she began to nudge it when she simply wanted to go out. Then, when Abe, the larger dog, had a bone or other treasure, Ellie began to nudge the door knob with what appeared to be a sneakier plan. When we opened the door, Abe would leap up to follow Ellie out. Almost immediately, we would hear scratching at the door. When we opened it, Ellie would rush in and capture the prize.

If the ability to reason is essentially the ability to solve problems, then I cannot see how we can deny Ellie some elements of rationality.

I could appeal to more objective research into animal intelligence, but the chances are excellent that you already agree. I don't really need to persuade you that dogs or chimps or dolphins or whales have experience. It isn't my purpose right now to talk about the ability of those other animals to solve problems, use language or tools, or otherwise show abilities similar to ours. Nor am I currently exploring the difficult question of animal rights or the use of animals for food or medical experiments or our other moral responsibilities. I just want you to think seriously about what it means to believe that all these creatures have experience of some kind.

How far down does experience go?

As obvious as it is that dogs or whales have experience, it is impossible to imagine with any accuracy what their experience is like. Indeed, I don't know what it is like to be *you*, much less what it is like to be my dog. But it is surely like something.[2] This difficulty increases as we move to animals that we have less personal interaction with, like rabbits and squirrels. Still, once we have taken the first step, what possible grounds could we have for denying experience to these animals? After all, the animals we have discussed so far have brains and central nervous systems with nerve endings and pain centers very much like ours. Both biologically and behaviorally, the evidence seems overwhelming that they share some forms of experiences that we also share, even though they almost certainly don't have the same abilities to do abstract thinking. To be more accurate, chimps and some other animals probably have a level of problem-solving abilities present in very young human children. Or, to be fair, they are only as good as young human children at solving the kinds of problems humans like for them to solve. They are obviously far better at solving problems about survival in their own environments than most humans would be.

So far I am expecting most people to agree that we human beings are not the only animals to have experience. The flight of imagination and the ability to test our imagination against facts become more difficult as we consider simpler animals. What about insects? They lack the kind of brain and central nervous system of higher animals.

They don't respond in the same way to pain. Yet they show amazing social behaviors and even the ability to communicate. Bees "dance" in ways that appear to communicate to other bees in the hive the direction and distance of food. Ants use chemical odors to communicate information. All of this is well documented in scientific research. How far down does experience of some kind go?

EXPERIENCE ALL THE WAY DOWN?

At this point, we need to pause and discuss the words *experience*, *feeling*, and *emotion*. Whitehead wanted us to see a radically new vision of reality. For that purpose, we cannot settle for using old words with old meanings. Whitehead either had to create new words or make old words do things we are not used to having them do. As I warned you before, Whitehead told us that sometimes we must stretch words in order to use them in ways that stretch our own imagination. *Experience*, *feeling*, and *emotion* are among the words Whitehead stretched.

If, in using *experience*, *feeling*, and *emotion*, we confine ourselves to consciousness, then clearly they do not go all the way down. Consciousness probably depends on a brain and central nervous system. But even most of *our* feelings are not conscious. Our bodies are taking in an enormous amount of data in each moment, and only a tiny portion of that information is raised to the level of consciousness. A simple illustration of this is the fact that if you fall asleep in a dark, quiet place, you can be awakened if someone suddenly turns on bright lights, makes loud noises, or gives you a sharp poke. If you did not feel those things, they wouldn't awaken you. When they pass over into the level of conscious awareness, you awaken. We constantly have our sensory warning systems at work but remain unconsciousness of most of that experience until it registers as a threat or something else of importance. Consciousness is only a tiny tip of the iceberg of human experience, and, I am arguing, human feeling is only a tiny tip of the feeling that is present in the larger world.

So, I invite you to stretch the words *experience*, *feeling*, and *emotion* to do new work, to carry new meaning. I hope that I will not cheat by simply equivocating, by simply giving the words radically unconnected meanings and pretending that this has profound importance.

Rather, I hope to take the work that the words already do, the meaning they already have, and stretch it out. I hope to use them as metaphors legitimately appealing for an intuitive leap.

Let us land our airplane for a moment and see what solid ground we have to stand on. I am proposing simply that we stop viewing the human mind/soul/psyche as something supernatural and alien to the natural world. I am proposing that your soul is 100 percent natural. I am guessing that many readers will already take this as obvious, and I am hoping that many others will have been at least partly persuaded. If it is true that our mind/soul/psyche is completely natural, then the question is: How does our experience arise out of the physical world? Whitehead's answer is that feeling, in a strangely but appropriately stretched meaning, goes all the way down.

Now, get back on our airplane, take off, and imagine that single-celled animals had some kind of feeling. We cannot imagine what that experience is *like*. Surely it would be devoid of consciousness. Consciousness was probably lost far up the animal chain. We aren't conscious all the time. But what would it mean to imagine that some kind of feeling is present in single-celled organisms? We can test our imagination against the simple observations that amoebas actively seek out food and move away from danger. Is it possible that, when certain physical conditions are present to provide the extra stimulation, the cell generates a centralized experience of attraction or repulsion with some very distant analogy to our own but devoid of all the complexity and intensity that go with consciousness?

Consider that the seventeenth- and eighteenth-century philosophy that saw them *merely* as machines entirely devoid of experience might be mistaken. Perhaps amoeba have, at an incredibly simple level, something that, in increasingly complex organisms, becomes the kind of experience that we see in dogs and chimps and dolphins and that you find in yourself.

What, after all, is the alternative? If experience is not, in some sense, present all the way down, how does it get to be present in the animals where we clearly believe it to be present—or in ourselves? If we acknowledge that feeling is not a supernatural reality injected uniquely into human beings, then doesn't it make sense to see it as permeating the world in varying degrees? Doesn't it make more sense to think this than to see it as arising out of a totally nonexperiencing world?

Now comes the hardest part of our flight of imagination and discovery. Imagine that experience/feeling/emotion goes *all* the way down to subatomic particles. Imagine that electrons, protons, neutrons, and other subatomic "particles" are drops of spatial-temporal experience. They experience their physical relationships with the world around them as vectored emotions—feelings that drive them this way and that. Think of energy as the transmission of physical feelings.

I'm going to take the risk here of quoting a rather long and technical passage from Whitehead to give you some feel for his intent. Although his language is dense, read it over and try to apply it against your experience:

> The experience has a vector character, a common measure of intensity, and specific forms of feelings that convey that intensity. If we substitute the term "energy" for the conception of a quantitative emotional intensity, and the term "form of energy" for the concept of "specific form of feeling," and remember that in physics "vector" means definite transmission from elsewhere, we see that this metaphysical description of the simplest elements in the constitution of actual entities agrees absolutely with the general principles according to which the notions of modern physics are framed. (*PR* 116)

We already know that the word *particle* is a misleading carry-over from seventeenth- and eighteenth-century physics when atoms were thought of as little billiard balls. Today, we think of electrons as bundles of energy, or as waves, without clear, sharp location. We speak of gravitational fields and electromagnetic fields and of space as having shape. So, while keeping all of that language of physics, imagine what would happen if we *also* think of an electron as a bundle of spatial-temporal experience, as a drop of feeling of causal relationships in space-time. An electron, we imagine, is feeling (not consciously, of course) its physical relationship with all of the other bundles of energy/experience in the field of causal relationships—that is, in the whole world around it.

I assume that, if we were to stick to the language of energy and energy fields, this would all seem quite proper and familiar to readers with some knowledge of modern physics. Twentieth-century physics has already established this description of the world—after some very high-flying and tremendously speculative flights of imagination that were tested against experimental facts. So now we are simply thinking about all of that in a slightly different way. What would happen if we thought of these subatomic bundles of interconnected energy as bundles of experience, vectored emotions of spatial-temporal energy relationships, out of which higher levels of experience will be created in much the same way as higher orders of macrocosmic objects like dogs and people are built out of electrons and protons? I think what would happen is that we could finally leave behind the last vestiges of Cartesian dualism, finally leave behind a supernatural view of the human mind, and finally see ourselves as 100 percent natural instances of the larger world around us.

How do we test this theory? How do we land again on firm ground? Part of the answer will emerge as we continue this exploration in later chapters. As we add each part of the picture, you will be better able to see if the whole picture makes sense, whether it describes what it is like to be you in this world. But we can already do some testing right now. You experience. Your body experiences. Your body is physical. Your physical body is made of cells, which are made of molecules, which are made of electrons, protons, and neutrons, which are bundles of energy/experience bound together in spatial-temporal fields of causal relationships. How does experience arise in this physical world? If it does not go all the way down, how can it arise in a world whose basic constituents are totally devoid of experience? If it does go all the way down, it seems unsurprising that, as these elementary drops of feeling are organized into successively more complex forms, like molecules and cells and animal bodies, central nervous systems and brains, the complexity of those feelings will increase until it crosses a crucial threshold into conscious self-awareness such as you are having right now. It would also explain why, as Whitehead observes:

> Consciousness flickers; and even at its brightest, there is a small focal region of clear illumination, and a large penumbral region of experience which tells of intense experience

> in dim apprehension. The simplicity of clear consciousness is no measure of the complexity of complete experience. Also this character of our experience suggests that consciousness is the crown of experience, only occasionally attained, not its necessary base. (*PR* 267)

Consciousness is only a tiny, but brilliant, flicker in the sea of experience that constitutes this world.

SOME CLARIFICATIONS ABOUT ROCKS AND MINDS

Let me clarify an important point: Rocks don't feel pain. Experience is something that only individuals have. An electron is probably an individual; a rock is not. Possibly atoms and molecules might be said to be complex individuals. Cells certainly appear to be individuals in this sense because they are organized to have a unity of structure and experience that enables them to interact with their environment in purposeful ways. Your mind is an individual. The point here is that rocks and chairs and pens don't have experience any more complex than that of the individual electrons or molecules that compose them.

Rocks don't have experience as rocks because they aren't organized that way.[3] Complex animal bodies like yours are organized precisely to channel experience and organize it into a single individual who is able to achieve awareness and direct the whole organism away from harm and toward food, etc. This individual experiencer, which draws together the vast wealth of experience of the cells composing your body, is your mind. If the connecting chains of nerve cells and brains cells that make this possible are disrupted, you stop being able to do this integrating. Whitehead speculated that trees and other plants do not have centralized experience because they don't have any central organ of perception or cognition. They don't have brains, so the experience of a tree is only the experience of its individual living cells. He saw plants as "democracies," while higher animals and human beings are more like "monarchies" with a "presiding personality" (*PR* 108–9).[4] He acknowledged the speculative character of such distinctions, but we can see his clear reasons for doing so.

The idea that experience goes all the way down—is present

throughout the natural world—is not at all like the idea that the world is the dream of some single dreamer, like God. Rather, the world is composed of an infinite number of individual drops of feeling, all woven together by their experiences of each other.

A further clarification about the relationship between mind and body will probably be helpful here. Descartes was wrong in his basic dualism. The world is not composed of substances or of two kinds of substances. There is, however, what David Ray Griffin calls an "organizational duality."[5] Descartes was correct that rocks and chairs and other large physical objects do not have minds, while humans do. In Whiteheadian terms, rocks are simply not organized to produce any level of experience above that of the molecules that form them. In living organisms, however, there can be varying degrees to which the organism is structured to give rise to a single series of feelings that can function to direct the organism as a whole. We can see fairly clearly that at least higher animals like chimps and dogs have a psyche (mind or soul) that is in many ways like our own. This psyche draws experience from the whole body (with varying degrees of directness and clarity), often crossing a threshold into some degree of consciousness, and is able in turn to use that awareness to direct the organism toward actions that help it to survive and achieve some enjoyment of life. The self, or soul, then is not something separate from the body. It arises out of the life of the body, especially the brain.

The mind/soul/psyche is the flow of the body's experience. Yet your body produces a unique mind that is also able to have experiences reaching beyond those derived directly from the body. We can think about philosophy, love, mathematics, or death in abstract conceptual ways that are not merely physical perceptions. Without the body, there would be no such flow of experience, but with a properly organized body, there can be a flow of experience that moves beyond purely bodily sensation. Furthermore, your mind can clearly interact with your body so that you can move, play, eat, hug, and work. There is a kind of dualism here in that the mind is not *only* the body but it is, in Griffin's phrase, a hierarchical dualism rather than a metaphysical one. There are not two kinds of substances—minds and bodies. There is one kind of reality—experience. But experience has both its physical and mental aspects.

SO WHAT?

The idea that experience goes all the way down, that it extends throughout nature, has powerful implications for the way we think about the world and ourselves. As I argued above, I think that Whitehead's vision allows us to leave behind the last vestiges of Cartesian dualism with its supernatural view of the human mind. Whitehead enables us to see ourselves as 100 percent natural instances of the larger world around us.

At the end of chapter 3, I said that acknowledging our full embodiment does not mean denying the wonderful range of experiences that we usually think of as spiritual. Rather, it means broadening our vision of the spiritual to include the physical and seeing value where we have not seen it before. If feeling is the root of the spiritual, then the flight we have taken in this chapter should suggest a very large sense of the spiritual indeed.

Whitehead's vision has tremendous ethical consequences. If we feel compassion for those who can suffer, then surely we must cast our net widely to reconsider who and what is worthy of our compassion. We can perceive the importance of treating other living things well for their own sakes, not just because they are useful to humans.

Much of our modern cruelty toward animals, especially in medical research, is rooted in a Cartesian view that animals have no experience and no souls. We obscure their capacity to suffer, so we can pretend that what we do to them in laboratories and hog lots does them no real harm. If animals have no experience and feel no pain or pleasure, then their lives can have no value *for them*. They only have value *for us*, and we are free to do with them as we wish. Immanuel Kant was quite clear that we have ethical obligations only to rational beings; hence, we have no ethical obligations to animals. We are free to use them entirely as means to our own ends. As a consequence, we are in the midst of one of the earth's great mass extinctions. Thousands of species are dying out because of our folly and our lack of concern for creatures other than our own species.

A process-relational vision of this world of experience calls us to a wider ethical responsibility toward all creatures. Animals have value *for themselves*, as well as for us. Consequently, we have ethical obligations toward them. It is obvious that process-relational thinkers lean toward the vision of John Stuart Mill, the nineteenth-century philosopher who insisted that actions are right or wrong not because of some abstract duty but because they have consequences for people's lives. Actions are right as they tend to make life better and wrong as they tend to make life worse. Mill emphasized that ethical obligations arise because of a creature's capacity for pain and pleasure. Process-relational thinking gives even greater depth and force to Mill's vision that we have obligations not only to human beings, "but, so far as the nature of things admits, to the whole sentient creation."[6] But even on the narrow vision of Immanuel Kant, there is room to include more than humans. If we accept that "reason" is best understood as a capacity for solving problems and if we examine the large and growing evidence that virtually all animals solve problems in the course of survival, Kantians may also find in process-relational thought a greater incentive toward insisting on the rights of animals.

LOOKING AHEAD

Understanding ourselves and the world as composed of experience will open the door to a much clearer and deeper vision of our own interwovenness with each other, with nature, with all of reality. Remember the Hindu and Buddhist image I mentioned in chapter 3, of the self as a drop of water in the ocean of reality. If the world is composed of experience, then the experiences that constitute your body and your mind are truly drops of the same "stuff" that constitutes the ocean of the world. There are no absolute boundaries between you and the rest of the world, yet your experience is still yours. We need to think further about this interweaving of self and world. Furthermore, "stuff," as I noted above, is clearly a very poor word since experience is neither "stuff" nor "things." It is dynamic and flowing. The traditional Cartesian language of "substance" simply cannot capture what experience is all about. In the next chapter, we will explore both of these themes.

Reality as Relational Process 5

SUBSTANCE AND PROCESS

All things flow.

—ALFRED NORTH WHITEHEAD, *PROCESS AND REALITY,* CITING HERACLITUS

SINCE YOU ARE an instance of the nature of things, we can learn from you something about the rest of the world. If the world is built of experience, we come back to the question: What is it like to be you? What is the nature of the flow of experience that is you? Let us take off in another airplane flight, basing imagination on the facts of your own experience.

Presumably, you remember your past, anticipate your future, and are experiencing your present. The present, of course, never stands still. Have you ever tried to make your experience stand still, to hold a single thought? Keep it simple. Think of a name, a number, a color, an image, and try to hold it for one minute. There is the moment of choosing, of starting, of holding, of being aware that this is hard, of thinking about your thinking about it, and so forth. A Hindu or Buddhist monk who has practiced many years at meditation can stay focused much longer, but there is still the beginning of meditation, the changing flow of meditation—breath in, breath out—and the end of meditation. Most of us will find our thoughts wandering long before a single minute has passed.

You, of course, already know that your experience flows. Your childhood is behind you, and you know that however much you may achieve a youthful frame of mind, you cannot bring back the years that have passed. Indeed, the present can happen only because those events have passed. The flow of life, of reality, is the flow of time. Only in the river of time, in the creative passage of events, can there be any life, history, or tradition, any achievement and enjoyment of value at all. But the swirling and crashing waves of that river inevitably draw all achievements back into the flow.

We need to be clear that, when we discuss time here, we are not talking about the artificial conventions of time that humans create—like seconds, minutes, and hours. Nor are we talking about some mysterious kind of absolute time within which events happen. Process philosophers, like modern physicists, reject the Newtonian view that time and space exist as some fixed background or framework separate from the events that happen within them as if time and space form a bottle around us that would still exist even if all events disappeared. Time simply *is* the passage—the becoming and perishing—of events.

What is it like to be you experiencing this becoming and perishing of moments? I have said that you remember the past, at least some of it. I would go further and ask if you do not also feel yourself arising out of your past. In the larger picture, you can see your present self as the product of all of your life experiences and decisions. But, more pressingly, do you not *feel* yourself as arising out of your immediate past, out of your experience of just a moment ago? If you stub your toe, don't you feel your reaction arising out of the experience of the pain? If a friend hugs you, don't you feel your emotions arising out of the experience of the hug—and all the relationship that went before? If someone treats you unfairly, don't you feel your emotional reaction rise out of that treatment?

Experience is always experience *of something*. That something becomes part of—actually constitutes—the experience. It is impossible for experience to exist independently: Experience arises out of that which is lived. That which is experienced from "outside" us becomes "inside" us, or better, becomes part of us because it is taken up into our self as experiencer. Every drop of experience is a novel weaving of the world of preceding experiences out of which that drop arises. The many experiences constituting the world of the past are brought together into a new experience. "It lies in the nature of things that the many enter into complex unity" (*PR* 21). The many become one. But there are many experiences arising in each new moment, so each "one" is also a part of the new "many." "The many become one, and are increased by one " (*PR* 21).

If this is true, and if it is also true, as I argued before, that your mind, or soul, is 100 percent natural, then what is a soul or mind? Your soul (mind or psyche) simply *is* the current cumulative flow of your experience. That answer may seem obvious to some, but it may become clearer to others if we consider some traditional ideas that Whitehead helps us move beyond.

The idea that the soul is supernatural often leads people to think of it as something separate from everything natural about themselves: separate from their bodies, separate from their experiences, possibly even separate from their emotions. The soul is often reduced to something static, detached, unaffected by the passage of events. After all, as we understand the natural causes of these things, as we understand more about how the brain generates thoughts, emotions, and experiences through purely natural processes, it seems necessary to separate the soul from all of them to preserve belief in its supernatural character.

René Descartes is helpful here again. Descartes (drawing on Aristotle) thought of the world as composed of *substances*. By substance, Descartes did not mean elements like wood or metal. He was thinking of particular concrete things like a rock, a mug, a human body—or an individual human mind like yours. We have already discussed his dualistic view that there are two kinds of substances: minds and bodies. But there are some features that Descartes believed all substances (mental and physical) have in common. (1) Substances exist independently of other substances. Descartes wrote, "By substance, we can understand nothing else than a thing which so exists that it needs no other thing in order to exist."[1] (2) Substances are also those unchanging realities that stand under (hence, sub/stance) their qualities and endure unchanged through the changes of those qualities.

Descartes asked us to consider a piece of solid white wax. The piece of wax has size, shape, color, and scent. If you thump it, it may give off a flat sound. If you melt the wax, it will become a clear liquid with none of its original qualities. Yet, we understand that it is the same wax. The substance—the wax—has endured through the changes of all of its qualities. We could go on to illustrate his explanation that the substance (wax) exists independently by imagining that the rest of the world has been destroyed and that this single piece of wax is drifting in empty space. It seems to require nothing but itself to exist just as it is.

Alfred North Whitehead points out the close connection between the substance/quality view of reality and the subject-predicate structure of our language. Loosely, when we say, "The wax is white," etc., "wax" is the subject of the sentence, and "white," "hard," and "smells like honey," are qualities or predicates. The term *wax* can remain fixed in the sentence regardless of how we substitute predicates. Grammatically, the phrase *the wax* exists independently of and endures unchanged through changes in predicates or qualities.

Consider the example of a pencil, and the sentence "The pencil is [or has, etc.]. . . ." The pencil is eight inches long, is painted blue, has gold letters on it, has a new eraser and a metal band, has a sharp point, etc. Philosophers sometimes refer to this list of qualities or predicates as "accidents," in the sense that the pencil just happens to be so long, blue, have an eraser, etc. Any of these accidental qualities could change, and we would still say it is the same pencil. The phrase *the pencil* seems to refer to some real entity, substratum, or substance that "stands under" all those accidents.

If we wear the eraser down, we still call it the same pencil. When the point becomes dull, we say it is the same pencil; it is just dull now. We sharpen the pencil so that it is now only seven-and-a-half inches long. It breaks, and we sharpen it again to seven inches. We still call it the same pencil. Perhaps we scrape off the blue paint and gold letters. Still the same pencil. Then we break it in half. We might pick up either half and still call it the "same" pencil. But "same" is beginning to strain.

Suppose we add, "The pencil is made of wood with a graphite core." Are wood and graphite simply accidental qualities? If we carefully remove the graphite core and replace it with another, is it still the same pencil? What if we remove the wood and replace *that* with plastic? More clearly, what if we simply remove all of these "accidental" qualities? What is left? *The pencil?*

Grammatically, the subject of the sentence, *the pencil*, can remain unchanged through all the changes of the predicates. Obviously, our grammar works like this because it is very useful for dealing with objects in the world around us.

> The simple notion of an enduring substance sustaining persistent qualities, either essentially or accidentally, expresses a useful abstract for many purposes of life. But whenever we try to use it as a fundamental statement of the nature of things, it proves itself mistaken.... But it has had one success: it has entrenched itself in language.... (*PR* 79)

We have here an important case in which the "common sense" of our culture is expressed in our language in a way that leads us to assume that the structure of language is the structure of reality. Some philosophers, like Descartes, seem to have accepted this identity between language and reality without sufficient question. Whitehead quotes John Stuart Mill's remark that such thinkers "thought that by determining the meaning of words they could become acquainted with facts" (*PR* 12). Further reflection will show that the world is far more complex.

A simple way to see this complexity is to think of the subject term of a sentence as shorthand for all of the predicates. *Wax* is just a simple way to refer to that cylinder over there that is heavy, white, smells of honey, etc. Viewed this way, we can see that every time the predicates change, the meaning of "wax" has changed. If we took away all the predicates there would simply be nothing left. The wax does not exist independently of the predicates/qualities: It simply *is* the sum of them taken together. As they change, the wax changes because it *is* the qualities. There simply is no mystical, invisible, enduring stuff that "stands under" all of those qualities and remains if we take them all away.

Apply this thinking to yourself. Begin with your body. Make a list of predicates—qualities—that describe you physically. You are so tall, weigh so much, have arms and legs, hands and feet, eyes, ears, a nose, etc. If we change one or two, the rest may remain so that we can still recognize you. But if we take away all of the parts (qualities) that are your body, there will obviously be nothing left. Your body simply is all of those parts together, changing as its parts change.

Finally, think of the flow of your own experience. Consider all of your memories, your sensory perceptions, your other feelings of bodily awareness of hunger, thirst, or caffeine jitters, your emotions, the words you are reading and thinking. It takes only a little attention to realize how rapidly these change. Some last only a moment and are gone forever. Some are recurring; you think of them many times over the years. You are aware, however, that even those long-standing memories change with time, as does the way you tell them and the way you feel about them. And, of course, most memories fade rapidly and are lost.

Stability is a relative matter in the flow of experience and never absolute. Many of these experiences and personality features could change—as they obviously do—and still leave you and those who know you with a clear sense that you are still you. But sometimes massive changes—like religious conversion, trauma, brain damage or diseases like Alzheimer's—can create such massive change that we say things like, "I don't even recognize myself anymore" or "She just isn't the same person I use to know."

Most clearly of all, if you take away all of those qualities, there is simply nothing left. You are a bundle of qualities, and a dynamic, changing bundle at that. Some qualities in that bundle are more persistent than others, but there is no unchanging "self," no mental substance that endures unchanged through the changes of qualities or that exists independently of those qualities so as to remain if they were all taken away. At this point, Whiteheadians are closer to the Buddhist view of "no-self" or *anatman* than to the Hindu view of the *atman* as an indestructible self.

The Scottish philosopher David Hume drove this point home. He asserted that the mental self is "nothing but a bundle or collection of different perceptions, which succeed each other with an inconceivable rapidity, and are in a perpetual flux and movement."[2] His argument was simple. Hume was an empiricist, a philosopher who insists that all knowledge of what exists must begin with experience. Consequently, he pointed out that, if we are to have any knowledge of or reason to believe in an unchanging self, we must have some experience of it. "If any impression gives rise to the idea of self, that impression must continue invariably the same, through the whole course of our lives; since self is supposed to exist after than manner. But there is no impression constant and invariable . . . and consequently there is no such idea."[3] Hume argued further that

> For my part, when I enter most intimately into what I call myself, I always stumble on some particular perception or other, of heat or cold, light or shade, love or hatred, pain or pleasure. I never can catch myself at any time without a perception, and never can observe anything but the perception. When my perceptions are removed for any time, as by sound sleep, so long am I insensible of myself, and may truly be said not to exist.[4]

Thus, Hume described the idea of an unchanging substantial self as a "fiction."[5]

We would do better, Hume argued, to think of rivers. We all know very clearly that rivers change constantly. We understand the term *river* to refer precisely to a flow of water that never remains the same. We ought to think in the same way about the bundles of qualities composing the rest of the world, and especially about ourselves.

You *are* the flow of your experience. Your mind, your soul, your psyche is that flow. Your sense of identity in that flow comes from memory and anticipation. There is a chain of experience out of which you arise, in each moment, more directly than does anyone else. You feel that as your own past, and you anticipate that the decisions you make in the present will shape a series of future experiences that will, in turn, be created out of this historical chain. The cumulative flow of psychophysical experience, including your own decisions shaping that series, is who you are. It is your mind, psyche, soul, your self.

Even Descartes sometimes acknowledged this dynamic and non-substantial character of the mind. He said that your mind (psyche or soul) is a "thing that thinks." "'I am, I exist' is necessarily true every time it is uttered by me or conceived in my mind." But what happens if there is no thought, no experience? "I am; I exist; this is certain. But for how long? For as long as I think. Because it could also come to pass that if I should cease from all thinking I would then utterly cease to exist."[6] Even Descartes, the father of our modern substance-quality vision of reality, recognized in some moments that the self is purely a bundle or flow of experiences.

The idea that the mind exists independently of its accidental experiences is difficult to escape because this idea is preserved in our ordinary language. We usually say that "I am *having* an experience." Those habits of language shape habits of thought. But you are reading this book precisely to consider thinking in other ways. So, explore the idea that Descartes hinted at but that Whitehead seized upon and developed, the idea that your mind (psyche or soul) simply *is* your flow of experience. More precisely, your mind or soul is the *cumulative* flow of your experience. You have a sense of self because of this continuity. You arise out of your past, out of your relationships with the whole world, and enjoy a momentary present that includes anticipation of future experiences. That moment becomes and perishes and gives birth to a new moment, which recreates you, with both continuity and novelty.

Novelty is essential for our survival. If we never changed, we would die. Novelty is the root of life. In expressing his rejection of the idea of a substantial self that endures unchanged through change, Whitehead looked more deeply at the character of life as novelty:

> We ask for something original at the moment, and we are provided with a reason for limiting originality. Life is a bid for freedom: an enduring entity binds any one of its occasions to the line of its ancestry. The doctrine of the enduring soul with its permanent characteristics is exactly the irrelevant answer to the problem which life presents. That problem is, How can there be originality? And the answer explains how the soul need be no more original than a stone. (*PR* 104)

Life is a balance between order and novelty. In that flow of experiences and decisions, a certain persistent personality is shaped. Without some continuity "depth of originality would spell disaster for the animal body" (*PR* 107). There are dominant characteristics, which are usually inherited and reiterated, a personality that we recognize in ourselves (or others) over time. That personality is shaped by your bodily inheritance, including your genes and other factors about your body, by your relationships with other people, and by your own decisions. As Aristotle and others have pointed out, character is shaped by decisions that become habits. The self that has these habits is known only in the flow of experiences, decisions, and actions, not in something mysterious that underlies them.

YOU AND THE WORLD

We have worked from the assumption that, in some important and very basic respects, what is true of you is true of everything in the world. You are part of the world, an example of it, not an exception to it. So what if an electron is like your mind? We can think of an electron not as an unchanging substance but as a series of electron events, each of which inherits from the entire past world but especially from its own immediate series of electron events. An electron, like you, would be a cumulative series of events, a flow of experience with both stability and novelty. The novelty open to an electron would be trivial compared to the complexity of a human mind, but there would still be both order and novelty. Surely this picture of an electron is far more consistent with all we know about electrons as waves and quantum events than would be the substantialist vision of reality. In that case, you and the electron and the whole universe made up of electrons and other elementary "particles" (such a bad name for them) would be a world of events, a world of relational processes.

Plato said that the world of time "is a process of becoming and perishing and never really is" (*Timaeus*, cited in *PR* 82). Plato believed that what is fully real is a realm of eternal and unchangeable forms that exists independently of the physical world. Like Descartes, Plato gave priority to being over becoming. The realm of becoming "never really is." Process philosophers recognize the importance of the language of being, but find deeper wisdom and greater clarity in a vision of the world as becoming, as relational process.[7] What "never really is" is the alleged "substance" that "stands under" all of the change, existing independently from it and enduring unchanged through all of the change. What *is* are events and relationships that constitute the process of becoming and perishing. The ordinary objects that we live among, which we see, feel, and touch, as well are our minds, are simply more or less stable "societies" of such relationships and events.[8]

SO WHAT?

The tension between our relational nature and the Cartesian idea of a self that endures unchanged through change is not confined to Western culture. At the end of chapter 10, I will lift up the positive dimension of the Hindu vision of compassion expressed in the Bhagavad Gita, but here I want to look at the more Cartesian side of Hindu thought in concept of the *atman*. The *atman* is that very Cartesian drop of unchanging divine reality that exists in each human being and is reincarnated from body to body. While there is much that is beautiful about this Hindu vision, it also has very troubling ethical implications, as can be seen in the famous Hindu scripture the Bhagavad Gita.

Arjuna, a member of the warrior class, is awaiting a great battle in which he must fight his own kinsmen. He confronts a moral dilemma between his duty as a warrior to fight and the wrongness of killing kin. Fortunately, Krishna, a God, an avatar of Vishnu, is there to consult. Krishna explains why Arjuna can do no harm by killing his kinsmen. If you can do no harm (or good), it is foolish to worry about consequences!

> There was never a time when I did not exist, nor you, nor any of these kings. Nor is there any future in which we shall cease to be.
> Just as the dweller in this body passes through childhood, youth and old age, so at death he merely passes into another kind of body. The wise are not deceived by that. . . .
> No one has power to change the Changeless.
> Bodies are said to die, but That which possesses the body is eternal. It cannot be limited, or destroyed. Therefore you must fight. . . .
> Know this Atman
> Unborn, undying,
> Never ceasing,
> Never beginning,
> Deathless, birthless,
> Unchanging for ever.
> How can it die
> The death of the body?

Knowing It birthless,
Knowing It deathless,
Knowing It endless,
For ever unchanging,
Dream not you do
The deed of the killer,
Dream not the power
Is yours to command it.[9]

While there is something deeply appealing in this vision of a soul as entirely safe from the ravages of the world, it strikes me as terrifying to suggest that it does not matter if we kill people since we cannot really kill them. War does no harm. Arjuna had argued that he should not kill his kin because it would have tragic consequences. If we start killing our kin, we destroy our families, and, hence, we destroy all of society. Krishna seems to argue that ethics is a purely individual matter of our own karma. Consequences (fruits) do not matter. The impression might easily be left that the way we treat other people has consequences for us but not for them. This is an ethical position that process-relational thinkers soundly reject. Gandhi, too, expressed concern over the literal message of Krishna's argument.

I hasten to add that the larger vision of the Gita certainly does not support this very troubling implication of the passage above. As we shall see later, other passages emphasize compassion and working for the common welfare. But insofar as the argument focuses on the vision of a self as an eternal enduring substance unharmed by the ravages of time and the physical world, it illustrates powerfully the concerns I am raising here.

Occasionally I have the pleasure of performing a wedding ceremony. As a process-relational thinker, I have something I want to say about human relationships in general, and marriage in particular.

As John B. Cobb Jr. wisely observed, a soul is not a thing.[10] It is not an isolated stone hidden somewhere inside us untouched by our life's experience, enduring unchanged by the changes of our lives. A soul is a dynamic process, a bundle of experiences, thoughts, emotions, dreams, and memories. In each moment of our life, we take in all of our past experience and all of our new experiences, and we create ourselves out of them, deciding who we will be in that moment.

Two people who join in marriage will be creating themselves out of each other and out of their relationship. Each word, each glance, each touch, each kiss, each shared moment, each thought about each other—everything they do will become part of the material out of which they will create themselves. They will gradually discover that they have literally become parts of each other, parts of each others' souls. They should have a special care, then, how they treat each other, have a care what material they each give to the other for the creation of their souls.

Obviously, a relational vision of the human soul confirms and helps to clarify our special obligations to children. A child's soul is not a supernatural Cartesian substance "which so exists that it needs no other thing in order to exist."[11] I'm sure Descartes never meant to suggest this, but if he were right about mental substances, it would seem to follow that it would not matter what experiences a child had. Whippings, cigarette burns, dark closets, verbal humiliation like "you're garbage and you always will be garbage" would just be so many accidental qualities that would come and go without changing that unchanging substance. But we know better. Process-relational thought offers us a vision of reality that helps us to understand what we all deeply know to be true. Sadly, as well as happily, we know that children must create themselves out of their relationships. They create themselves out of the genes and the nutrition and love, neglect, or cruelty they receive. They must create their souls out of the relationships they find themselves in. While there is some degree of self-creative freedom that often allows children to amaze us with their resilience, every person who has ever talked to me about the impact of abuse on them speaks of the deep scars they carry and will always carry. Children create their souls out of their relationships with us. Have a care: It matters what we give them to work with.

LOOKING AHEAD

In the next chapter, we will begin to understand more about the dynamic character of these relationships. What holds the world of events together, and what creates rich novelty in our lives?

Reality as a Causal Web 6

A CONSTRUCTIVE POSTMODERNISM

Also in our experience, we essentially arise out of our bodies which are the stubborn facts of the immediate relevant past. We are also carried on by our immediate past of personal experience; we finish a sentence because *we have begun it.*

—ALFRED NORTH WHITEHEAD, *PROCESS AND REALITY*

WHAT HOLDS the world of dynamic, novel events together in an orderly cosmos? What connections enable the flow of experience that constitutes an electron or your mind to have identity over time? We have repeatedly seen that each moment of existence arises out of previous moments. As we take flight once again, we spiral back to that theme to discover yet another vital contribution of process-relational thought.

Contemporary postmodern thinkers often speak of truth and values and even of our most basic perceptions as social constructs. They tend to emphasize the disconnectedness of these social constructs from the alleged world "out there," almost as if there were no world at all but only the worlds we construct. How might process-relational thinkers respond?

Postmodern thinkers of many kinds, including feminists, liberation theologians, Marxists, and pragmatists have done us all valuable service. They have shown us how structures of social oppression falsely acquire an air of absoluteness that serves to make oppression seem "natural," as if it were part of the necessary structures of reality. Instead, they argue, these social values, gender roles, and often our very sensory experiences are social and personal constructs. These critiques have played important roles in greater social liberation for women, people of color, the poor, and people with different sexual orientations.

Unfortunately, in the process of helping us to see the constructed character of our perceptions, some postmodernists seem at times to deny that we have any real connection to the world "out there." Sometimes it may seem as if there is no natural world out there, as if there is *only* the constructed political and social world they critique.

Whitehead offers a valuable contribution to this contemporary conversation that can help us to retain the liberating wisdom that points to the constructed character of our experience while simultaneously weaving us back into the world in which we are inescapably enmeshed. To understand Whitehead's contribution, let me begin with some historical perspective.

The philosopher David Hume, who helped us clarify the nature of the self as a bundle of experiences, was a British empiricist. In the spirit of the Renaissance, the British empiricists emphasized the importance of going out to look at the world. They rejected the idea that we are born with innate knowledge and argued that all knowledge of what exists in the world depends upon experience. It is true, empiricists acknowledge, that we can learn purely rational processes of logic and math, but reason alone cannot tell us what *exists*.

Consider a simple mathematical truth like $1 + 1 = 2$. As a truth of reason, it is a purely logical and necessary truth. But reason alone does not tell us whether anything at all exists in the physical world or how the physical world behaves. If you take a drop of water on a surface and add another drop of water, how many drops will you have? It depends. If you drop some water from above, it might very well splash into many drops. If you set a drop very carefully alongside the first drop, you may end up with two drops—unless they touch. The problem is that the physical properties of water are not captured in the formula $1 + 1 = 2$. We have to look and see how water actually behaves.

We could appear to solve the problem by saying something like one drop of water added in the right way to another drop of water will give us two drops of water. In this sentence, what does "in the right way" mean? It can only mean something like "in a way guaranteed to give us two drops of water." Now we have turned the statement into a tautology, a necessary but trivial truth. Add one drop to another drop in a way that will give us two drops, and you will have two drops. As a logically necessary truth, it separates itself and us from the problem of how water actually behaves. As soon as we step back into the physical world, we have to see what happens when we add one drop to another drop in one way or another, and we may not get the same answer every time.

While we could explore many more examples, you can at least see why the British empiricists insisted that all knowledge of this world depends upon experience. Whitehead would agree with this basic claim: "The ultimate test is always widespread, recurrent experience" (*PR* 17).

The radical empiricism of Hume and others, unfortunately, was very narrowly focused on sense experience. Knowledge of the world was taken to depend on what we could see, touch, taste, hear, and smell. The final test of knowledge is usually what we see.

David Hume, however, discovered important difficulties raised by his own empiricism, and, being an honest thinker, he pointed them out to everyone. The principal difficulty related to causation. We cannot see (or otherwise sense) causation. We see event A followed by events B and C, but we do not see causation.

If you watch one billiard ball strike another billiard ball, you will then see them move off in different directions (usually), but you will not see causation. Watch as carefully as you can, and you will only see the series of events, not any causing of one by the other. You might protest, "Of course, I see causation. I see this ball cause that ball to move." But do you? Hume insisted that all you *see* is the sequence of events. You *assume* or *infer* that the earlier events cause the later ones, but all you *see* is the sequence.

When we look about us toward external objects and consider the operation of causes, we are never able, in a single instance, to discover any power or necessary connection, any quality that binds the effect to the cause and renders the one an infallible consequence of the other. We only find that the one does actually in fact follow the other. The impulse of one billiard ball is attended with motion in the second: This is the whole that appears to the *outward* senses. The mind feels no sentiment or *inward* impression from this succession of objects; consequently, there is not, in any single particular instance of cause and effect, anything that can suggest the idea of power or necessary connection.[1]

Being the extremely honest thinker that he was, Hume acknowledged that he had to work very hard to force himself to admit that he could not experience causation and that the moment he stopped making this mental effort, he immediately reverted to believing in it. Yet, he thought this strange psychological fact did not refute his argument. It just told us something interesting about our mental habits.[2]

Immanuel Kant, the great German philosopher, read Hume's work and reported that he was awakened from his "dogmatic slumbers." Hume was right: All experience about what particular things exist in the world is based on experience, but we cannot experience causality. Nor, Kant argued, can we experience space, time, or substance. Kant concluded that space, time, substance, and causality are simply ways in which our minds order our experience. They do not come from the world; they come from us. So while we cannot know about the specific content of the world until we go and look, we can know in advance that whatever experience we have will be shaped by our minds into these basic categories. A familiar analogy is that, if we wear rose-colored glasses, we cannot know in advance what we will see, but we can know in advance that whatever we see will appear rose colored.

Kant, therefore, distinguished between the noumenal world—the world as it is in itself—and the phenomenal world—the world as actually experienced by us. We cannot know anything about the noumenal world. All we will ever know is the world as we experience it—the phenomenal world. Yet, as many critics have asked, if we cannot know anything about the noumenal world, how can we know that it exists or that it does or does not include space, time, causality, and substance?

WHITEHEAD'S RESPONSE

Whitehead agreed that we must be empiricists since knowledge of the world derives from experience. He also agreed with Hume that our senses cannot show us causation. There is also something important and true in Kant's insistence that we can never step outside of our own experience to see what the world is like on its own.

Nevertheless, Whitehead argued, we do experience causation, as well as space and time (though obviously not substance). We experience these, however, at a deeper level than our sense experience. Whitehead distinguished between two kinds of perception: perception in the mode of causal efficacy and perception in the mode of presentational immediacy. The latter, presentational immediacy, is sense experience. Sense experience is rooted in the deeper perception in the mode of causal efficacy.

Consider sight. Sight is a sophisticated activity of the eyes, the optic nerves, and the brain. Photons strike the rods and cones of the eyes, and electrochemical messages are transmitted along the optic nerves to the rear of the brain. Reflex action can be derived from this. But from there, the cerebral cortex takes over and transforms that raw data into a conscious visual perception so that we see—and know that we are seeing—an apple on a table. It is possible, of course, that the brain will misinterpret signals it receives and we may experience an illusion, something that doesn't line up with what is actually going on "out there."

That complex visual experience created by the brain depends upon a causal interaction between the world "out there" and our eyes, an interaction that involves photons. Photons are bundles of energy that transmit energy to the rods and cones in our eyes. Sight, then, is certainly a product of our own organism, and the organism is capable of misinterpretation. It is true that we can never step outside of our bodily existence to know what is going on "out there" independently of our bodies, yet our bodies create sight out of a deeper causal interaction with the world. The same is true of all of our sense perceptions. All of them are products of the interaction—the relational process—of our organic lives with the causal world around us.

By now, of course, you are beginning to understand Whitehead's vision of the character of all becoming as relational processes. The whole universe, all that is actual, is composed of the becoming and perishing of moments of experience, experience of spatial-temporal relations and experiences of causal connections. Each moment arises causally out of the prior moments. Each moment in the life of a photon arises causally out of the previous moments in the life of that photon or the other events that produce that photon.

Whitehead argued that we believe in causation because we experience ourselves in each moment as arising causally out of the preceding moments. We believe in causation because we experience ourselves as part of a causal web. We discover that our sense organs do not always interpret that causal web appropriately, but we only discover that because we experience other causal forces that challenge such interpretations, as when we stumble over a step we did not see in the dark.

Experience in the mode of causal efficacy is shared by every drop of experience. Physicists describe these interactions in the language of energy, chemists in terms of chemical interactions, and biologists in terms of organic behavior. Electrons experience the causal force of the other events out of which they arise and respond. Amoebas experience their environment and respond to it. So do we. The world is a vast web of causal relationships—relational processes.

Every act of experience has its own unique perspective, its own "actual world." No two events arise out of exactly the same spatial-temporal situation. Much less do any two moments in a human life arise out of exactly the same context. Certainly, no two people share the same biography. Furthermore, each new experience involves interpretation of the received data. In our case, we interpret the impact of photons and the energy they convey in terms of sight. We interpret those sights in terms of memories, emotions, plans, hopes, fears, and possible reactions. So process philosophers agree emphatically with the contemporary postmodern awareness of the importance of perspective and interpretation. All experience is from a perspective, and all experience involves interpretation.

But—and this *but* is crucial—every experience has a perspective on the actual world, and every interpretation involves an interpretation of that world. Even if we are interpreting a fictional work like *Hamlet*, we are engaged in that interpretive act within the context of a broader experience of the actual world within which we read, think, discuss, attend plays, and explore ideas. Even our interpretation of the fictional is enmeshed in the lived experience of the actual.

Let's return to Whitehead's distinction between perception in the mode of presentational immediacy and perception in the mode of causal efficacy. It is a familiar fact that when we look at a star that is eight light years away we are seeing light that left that star eight years ago. Thus, we never see the star as it is right now; we always and only see it as it was in the past. This is true, of course, of every star in the sky. Our eyes take in light, and ours brains use it to paint the night sky with spots of light, and perhaps with a moon, constructed of our most recent perceptions. The stars, moon, and sun as we see them are always constructs of our brains, taking our most recent experience and painting the world with it. But this clearly does not deny the existence or causal impact of the stars, moon, and spatial fields in which we all exist.

What is true of the sky is equally true of the rest of the world. As I sit at my desk, gazing out the window while writing this, my brain uses visual, tactile, and other sensory input from my body to construct my visual and auditory (olfactory, etc.) world of the present. This constructed world of sensory "presentational immediacy" that allows me to find the computer and type, to look out the window and track a flying bird, or to smell something burning in the kitchen is a constructed presentation built from data about how the world impacted my body just a moment ago.

The paint my brain uses to create this presentation is my body's causal interaction with the world around me, as well as the causal interactions within my body. It is finally these more basic perceptions in the mode of causal efficacy against which we test our constructed presentation. We speak of illusions and delusions when our brains paint the world of presentational immediacy in ways not appropriately connected to its actual causal systems. So we ultimately test the painted world against the causal world. It is perception in the mode of causal efficacy that tells me that I cannot walk through walls, cannot flap my arms and fly, cannot engage the world as if it were entirely my own creation.

I push and the world pushes back. If I am struck, I feel the presentational immediacy of pain constructed by my nerves and brain, but I experience that pain *with* and arising out of the physical causal energy of what strikes me. A flying rock carries physical force, and that force is the ground of my sensory experience of the impact. I experience the pain *with* and *because of* that causal energy.

The world and I causally engage each other in each moment. My body arises out of this web of causal relations, and my mind arises out of the causal interactions of my body. In each moment, I experience myself—through perception in the mode of causal efficacy—as arising out of that causal web. That, Whitehead so persuasively argues, is why we all believe in causation. We believe in causation because we experience it in every moment of our becoming and experience ourselves in each moment as being caused by that past world. We cannot help but believe, at a deep, prereflective level, what we experience in each moment of our existence.[3]

Hume was honest. He was honest enough to admit that he did not *see* causation or know it by any sense experience. He was also honest enough to confess that, despite this philosophical insight, he could not help but believe in causation at a deeper level. Process philosophers have often been critical of Hume for excluding from his philosophy something he knew to be true just because it did not fit his conceptual framework; but we at least recognize that this exclusion arose because he lacked the conceptual framework of perception in the mode of causal efficacy and was honestly lost as to how to make sense of the world with the conceptual tools at his command.

Process thinkers would agree with Kant, and with many postmodern thinkers, that the world of our sensory perception is always a construct. To use Kant's language, the world of our sensory experience is a "phenomenal" world. The phenomenal world is the world our brain paints for us of sight, sound, taste, smell, and touch. The sensory world of our "now" is never identical with the world as it is in itself.

Kant had no way to connect this phenomenal world with what he called the "noumenal" world as it is in itself, a world he thought forever inaccessible to us, a world without space, time, or causality. Whitehead argued that the world "out there," the world "in itself" *does* have space, time, and causality and that we can know this because we experience ourselves as part of that larger causal world through perception in the mode of causal efficacy.

Understanding causal efficacy transforms discussions of contemporary postmodernism. Deconstructive postmodernists rightly emphasize the perspectival and constructed character of our experience of the world. But partly because of the heritage of Hume and Kant, they often leave us dangling as if there is simply no connection between our constructed phenomenal world and the world that we all *know* is "out there." Process-relational thought, especially through Whitehead's insight regarding our perception in the mode of causal efficacy, acknowledges much that is wise in current postmodernism while weaving us back into the world web and helping us conceptually to understand how we *know* that we are part of that world. We know it because we experience it in every moment of our lives. We construct our worlds and ourselves *out of* that larger world of causality. We experience the world "out there" because we create ourselves out of it. The world "out there" becomes part of us; it becomes the "in here."

A word needs to be said in response to an obvious and thoughtful line of questions that might be raised. How do we know? What do you mean? Show me an example.

William James pointed out that the last step at the bottom of the stairs is there whether we know it or not. Who among us has not felt the jarring physical impact with the ground that came earlier or later than we had expected—or when our mind was engaged on other matters? Who has not stubbed their toe and encountered the world pushing back?

Examples can be tricky, however. One colleague of mine cites a famous catch by Willie Mays. Standing in centerfield Mays saw the batter hit the ball. Seeing that it was a long one that was going to travel right over his head, Mays turned his back on the ball, sprinted away from home plate, and then, at the last moment, looked over his shoulder, reached out, and caught the ball in full stride. How did he know where the ball would be? Causal efficacy.

As delightful as it is, this is a tricky example. The colleague who tells this story doesn't mean that somehow Willy "felt" the ball's path through perception in the mode of causal efficacy, as if were a kind of sixth sense. That isn't Whitehead's claim. Whitehead's claim is that *all* of our experience is rooted in causal efficacy. We live and move within it. Hand-eye coordination is learned by the trial and error of causal engagement with baseballs, flying mosquitoes, computer keyboards, and lover's lips. It is this continually experienced causality that underlies all other experience by which we learn to engage the world around us and by which Willie Mays had learned to judge the path of that fly ball.

SO WHAT?

Feminists rightly show us that "gender" is a social construct enmeshed in struggles of power, wealth, class, and physical violence. Social constructs evolve over millennia, embedded in language, social practices, gender roles, religious ritual, and more. Hence, they carry tremendous weight in shaping our experience.

Sometimes, however, it seems as if overzealous people suggest that there is *only* the social construct. Admittedly, it is impossible for us to think about reality in any way not shaped by *some* social constructs. Yet, process-relational thinkers remind us that these social constructs, as deep as they are, are created *out of* our lived embodiment as biological organisms engaging in causal webs deeper than our social practices, languages, and concepts. The task is to attend to our deepest experience in ways that allow us to critique (admittedly from within) the very concepts we have inherited to think with.

Those of us who support feminist values and critiques will make more sense and speak more convincingly to people as we acknowledge and attend to our individual and shared experience of the causal physical/biological roots underneath all social constructs. It is, after all, the whole biological, social, psychological self of the battered wife, the abused child, and the disenfranchised woman who experiences the violently *causal* consequences of oppressive gender constructs.

Physical violence is always experienced within a social construct. But when a man's fist crashes into a battered woman's face, we all know that the event is not *only* a social construct. She experiences the pain as *caused by* the impact of fist on flesh and bone. There is physical, causal force in that impact out of which our nerves construct pain signals. But the force of the blow *is* that causal efficacy out of which her physical pain arises, and she *experiences* that causal force in the blow and the pain.

Because everyone knows this is true, forms of postmodernist feminism that neglect these lived experiences may serve to weaken feminist critiques of culture. Process-relational thinking affirms and deepens feminist and other liberationist critiques of social hierarchies, while rooting those critiques more effectively in ways that acknowledge and make sense of what we all experience.

More positively, and just as importantly, process-relational thinking affirms that love also has causal efficacy in the world. The flow of experience constituting your conscious and unconscious self—including your love for others—also participates in the causal web of life as both effect and cause. That means that your experience of love can move your hands and arms to touch with gentleness, to hug with protectiveness, to reach out to others in ways that enact the causal power of your love in the world.

LOOKING AHEAD

So far, our flights of imaginative construction have shown us a world rooted in immediate experience, a world of interrelated events and processes, a world in which minds and bodies are united, and a world in which causality is experienced in each moment of our existence. In our next flight, we will continue to see human beings living within the web of the whole world, but we will concentrate on a new vision of the meaning of power, especially as it is experienced in human relationships.

Unilateral Power 7

POWER, VALUE, AND REALITY

The definition of being is simply power.
—PLATO, *THE SOPHIST*

POWER, VALUE, and reality are tied together in our cultural traditions. That which is most powerful is often seen as the most valuable and also the most real. God is the clearest example. There is something very important in this relationship between power, value, and reality, but process thinkers argue that the relationship is sadly distorted in most religious, political, cultural, and philosophical visions.

Look at the world around you, and consider what most people would see as concrete examples of power. People I ask for models of power often identify winning sports teams. They may name Microsoft creator Bill Gates or the president of the United States. Or they may point to armies or nuclear weapons. Occasionally, someone will choose natural forces like hurricanes, tornadoes, and earthquakes.

What do all of these have in common that makes them "powerful"? Usually, people work toward the idea that power is the ability to affect others without being affected by them. A professional football team playing against a school team could score any time it wanted without being scored against. Bill Gates can tell anyone in his huge company what to do, but they can't tell him what to do—because he can fire them. The president of the United States can send armies around the world, armed with weapons of amazing destructive power, and can even order the firing of nuclear warheads that will kill tens of millions. The president, as we know, can do this even if millions of people all around the world march in the streets in protest. They cannot tell him (or possibly a future "her") what to do because he is the president of the United States. He has it in his power to destroy the world as we know it. That, people say, is real power: the ability to affect others without being affected by them. As one political theorist explains, "On the international scene I should define power as the capacity of a political unit to impose its will upon other units. [This entails both] *defensive power* (or the capacity of a political unit to keep the will of others from being imposed upon it) and *offensive power* (or the capacity of a political unit to impose its will upon others)."[1]

"Unilateral power" is the label applied to this traditional vision by the process philosopher and theologian Bernard Loomer.[2] To be unilateral here means to move one way. The president orders the generals and admirals. The generals and admirals command the captains. The captains direct those below them who ultimately control the seamen and privates. Orders flow one way—down the ranks. They don't move upward against the flow of power.

Of course, power is always limited by someone or something. Even the most powerful sports teams sometimes lose; even Bill Gates can be sued by the U.S. government. The most powerful army suffers casualties and can lose wars. The president can lose an election or be impeached, sailors can mutiny against captains, and kings must fear being assassinated by their barons. Simple clay resists the will of the potter. Still, our ordinary everyday sense of power is well captured in the idea that power is, within limits, the ability to affect others without being affected by them.

If power is unilateral, then it is competitive. If you have more power over me, I must have less power over you. More unilateral power for some means less for others. Those at the bottom of the heap—the poor, the abused child, the battered wife, the chained prisoner, the slave—are most vulnerable to suffering and death. It is obvious, then, why we all want unilateral power. We don't want to be pushed around, humiliated, fired, beaten up, raped, or murdered. We want to be in control of our own lives, and that means that we have to be able to resist the intrusions of others and assert our own will. Even the hermit seeks the power of seclusion, the power not to be bothered by others. It isn't only other people who have power, of course. We all worry about disease, old age, natural disasters, and death. The world surrounds us with natural power we have very limited power to resist. All the medicines, doctors, and storm cellars in the world won't guarantee us the power to resist the effects of the forces of nature that threaten us. The first noble truth of Buddhism is that all life involves suffering—and suffering at its root means being affected by the world around us. Since we don't want to suffer and we don't want to die, Friedrich Nietzsche saw life as a "will to power."

This powerful human impulse to protect ourselves at the expense of others—or at least to have the power to do so when we choose—is confirmed by a deep philosophical and theological tradition that also connects unilateral power with value and reality.

THE PHILOSOPHICAL TRADITION

Plato wondered about the nature of being. What does it mean for anything at all to *be*. He especially wanted to argue that ideas have being. So, in his dialogue *The Sophist*, Plato established one of the cornerstones of all Western thought by defining the nature of being.

> My notion would be that anything that possesses any sort of power to affect another, or to be affected by another, if only for a single moment, however trifling the cause and however slight the effect, has real existence; and I hold that the definition of being is simply power.[3]

Plato was right. There is no being without power, and power can be understood as both the ability to affect and the ability to be affected. The wrong turn, however, came because Plato and most other thinkers, from philosophers to theologians to kings, have believed that it is only the ability to affect that really counts, while the ability to be affected is largely a defect or weakness. Plato made his value judgment very clear.

> Things that are at their best are also least liable to be altered or decomposed.... Then everything that is good, whether made by art or nature or both, is least liable to suffer change from without.... But surely God and the things of God are

> perfect in every way? . . . Then it is impossible that God should ever be willing to change; being, as is supposed, the fairest and best that is conceivable, every God remains absolutely and for ever in his own form.[4]

The impact of Plato's vision of divine unchangeablilty on later Christian concepts of God was absolutely foundational. Plato's divine realities, however, were not gods but the eternal, unchangeable forms. Influenced by the model of mathematics, Plato argued that physical objects and actions in this world of change are merely more or less poor copies of those eternal forms. The connection between reality, value, and power is made clear in the fact that the highest of these forms is the form of the Good, followed closely by the forms of Truth, Beauty, Justice, and other virtues. These forms, Plato argued, are as eternal and absolutely unchangeable as are the geometric forms of circles, squares, and triangles. These eternal forms, whether mathematical or moral, are not gods who issue commandments, who are pleased or displeased by obedience or rebellion, or experience the passions of love or hate. Yet, they order the world by their very Being. Power, value, and Being are united in them. In contrast, Plato argued, the physical world is a realm of mere shadows, which flicker but have no real Being.

> What is that which always is and has no becoming; and what is that which is always becoming and never is? That which is apprehended by intelligence and reason is always in the same state; but that which is conceived by opinion with the help of sensation and without reason, *is always in a process of becoming and perishing and never really is*.[5]

Aristotle challenged Plato's vision in many important respects, including giving Being a more dynamic character. Nevertheless, he gave us one especially clear example of the traditional connection between unilateral power, value, and reality. Aristotle described his God as the Unmoved Mover. The whole world was affected by God, but God was affected by nothing. Obviously, the divine Unmoved Mover was unchangeable—just as Plato had argued. Aristotle saw that the immutability of the Unmoved Mover meant that God could have no knowledge of this world. The world changes; knowledge of change would create change in God. Besides, the world was not worth thinking about. So Aristotle's God eternally thought about God.

Obviously, René Descartes shared Plato's emphasis on unchanging Being by envisioning God and human minds as unchanging substances. To repeat Descartes' view: "By substance, we can understand nothing else than a thing which so exists that it needs no other thing in order to exist."[6] Strictly speaking, Descartes acknowledged, only God is a true substance, but finite substances can be said to exist independently of everything else save God. Descartes' substances, including human minds/souls, exist by virtue of their power to remain unaffected by change.

Gottlieb Wilhelm Leibniz reaffirmed the traditional valuation of active power over merely passive power: "A created thing is said to act outwardly insofar as it is perfect, and to suffer from another insofar as it is imperfect. Thus action is attributed to the Monad insofar as it has distinct perception, and passion or passivity insofar as it has confused perception."[7] He carried the logic of Descartes' idea of substances to the extreme by arguing that, since substances exist independently and endure unchanged, they must not have any effect on each other. Of course, this applies only to created substances, not to God, since God absolutely controls all created substances. Indeed, the appearance of causality and relationship in the world arises from the fact that God has created the universe with a "pre-established harmony," so that when a log splits while being struck by an ax, it would not be the ax causing it. Only God can actually cause anything. Monads (Leibniz's term for these solitary substances) "have no windows." They mirror the world around them because of the preestablished harmony, but nothing gets in. The world is totally devoid of any internal relationships.

John Locke, in his *Essay Concerning Human Understanding*, also reaffirmed the valuation of active power over passive power and pictured reality as a hierarchy of unilateral power.

> Power thus considered is two-fold, viz. as able to make, or able to receive any change. The one may be called active, and the other passive power. Whether matter be not wholly

> destitute of active power, as its author, God, is truly above all passive power; and whether the intermediate state of created spirits be not that alone which is capable of both active and passive power, may be worth consideration.[8]

The Western philosophical tradition illustrates the cultural dominance of our commitment to unilateral power as the ability to affect without being affected. Unilateral power is linked with value and reality. What is unilaterally powerful is what is valuable and real.

SO WHAT?

What does this mean in real life? Unilateral power is controlling and dominating. By idolizing it, we shape our entire culture. Whether in war or social oppression, we frequently justify cruelty to others by denying their full humanity. So far as we link power with reality and value, it is easy to create social structures in which the weak are seen as less valuable because less "really" human. The connection with traditional patriarchal hierarchy is glaringly evident. Men were to rule, to be aloof, to be governed by reason, not to cry. Women were seen as less rational than men, more emotional, and hence more easily affected (that is, weaker), were thereby ranked as less fully human than men and hence less valuable. Children were to be seen, not heard. Slaves, servants, employees, children, racial or ethnic minorities, the poor—all who were weaker were inherently less valuable, and somehow perhaps lacking in the reality of "Man."

Look at the world around you, and ask yourself where you find the purest examples of unilateral power. Where do you see one person or group of persons exercising the most fully unilateral power over other persons? Would we not find the very peak of unilateral power in torture chambers, slavery, rape, child abuse, murder, and the like? There is something deeply wrong here in seeing unilateral power as the essence of value and reality.

What is wrong can be seen clearly in the opposition between unilateral power and love. To be fully unilaterally powerful, I must not be affected by people, and that means I must not care about them. Healthy caring love is just the opposite: the more we love, the more we open ourselves up to being affected by the other. If we are not to say that love is inherently powerless, we need a new vision of power, a relational vision.

LOOKING AHEAD

I believe process-relational thinking has richly compelling resources for reshaping this fundamental dimension of human thought. Once again, we must take flight and try to rise above some of our most deeply seated cultural assumptions about how the world works, hoping to see something truer and better than what we have taken for granted. As always, however, we will be constantly checking our new vision against the immediate facts of our own experience. Here, again, I hope to make you say simultaneously both "Holy Cow!" and "Of course! That is how I really experience it."

Relational Power 8

SO WHAT?

The true good is an emergent from deeply mutual relationships.
—BERNARD LOOMER, "TWO KINDS OF POWER"

BREAKING with our usual format, this entire chapter is about the "so what?" of the relational vision.

It seems clear that it is precisely the power to be *affected* that increases as we move up the chain of complexity from mere electrons, to molecules, to microorganisms, to plants and animals, to vertebrates with brains and central nervous systems, and finally (so far as we know yet) to human beings. It is not our power to remain unaffected, or even the power to control others, that makes our lives richer and more valuable. It is our amazing capacity to be affected by the incredible richness and complexity of the relational web in which we live. Our capacities for pain and pleasure, our physical senses, our appreciation of beauty, our openness to ideas, and our ability to learn and adapt are the powers that distinguish us from electrons and rocks and microbes. In short, the higher we go toward more complex organisms, the more the power to be *affected* emerges.

Perhaps you are thinking, "Holy Cow!" and "Of course." While this fact can be clear to anyone, it also arises directly out of the process-relational vision of the world we have been exploring. Power, value, and reality go together. Plato was right that the definition of Being is simply power. But process-relational philosophy turns our understanding of power on its head in a way that can transform our vision of reality and of human relationships. As always, however, my argument will appeal first and foremost to your own experience and to your own knowledge of the world.

Let me digress from a direct discussion of Whitehead's thought to draw from one of his disciples, Bernard Loomer. Loomer first proposed that we distinguish between unilateral power and relational power. He wrote about relational power in terms of the two components of being affected and affecting others.[1] In my own formulation, relational power includes three components: (1) the ability to be actively open to and affected by the world around us; (2) the ability to create ourselves out of what we have taken in; and (3) the ability to influence those around us by having first been affected by them. Let us again take flight and imagine what the world would be like if people operated by this kind of power.

Process-relational thinkers like Loomer and Whitehead agree with Plato that everything actual exercises some power—either to affect or to be affected. But as you can anticipate, they reject the assumption that the peak of power is the ability to control others unilaterally while remaining unaffected by them. If you were completely unaffected by the world around you, you would simply cease to exist because you are constantly creating yourself out of your relationships with that world. There is a crucial, life-shaping difference between the kind of *weakness* that makes us vulnerable to being controlled by others and the *strength* that enables us to be active and open to the world around us. There is an equally vital difference between the power to control others while shutting them out of our lives and the power to engage the lives of others in ways that enrich us all.

Consider parenting. All too often, parents choose the path of unilateral power because it is easier than sharing power. This long cultural tradition, though now being challenged, is clear in familiar old sayings. Children are to be seen, not heard. Children are not to speak unless spoken to. Children must obey. If parents are wealthy enough, they may have shipped their children off to boarding schools early in life to keep them out from under foot. Physical punishment has been the norm through most of history. When children ask why they must do something, the answer is all too often, "Because I said so." If parents are too tired, too busy, too frazzled, too angry, too selfish, or perhaps just too lazy, "because" is an easy answer. "Because" is an especially attractive answer when we have no better reason for our commands.

For thousands of years, children have inherited this unilateral model of parenting and have passed it on. They have carried it into their marriages, their parenting, their roles as bosses, politicians, generals, rapists, and child abusers. The idea seems to be that children have to take the abuse now, but the payback will come when they are adults and they get to abuse others.

I have seen other models of parenting, and I hope you have, too. I have seen parents and other care providers who listen with patience and active openness, who work at understanding how the world looks through their children's eyes, ears, and emotions. I have seen parents who shape their parenting decisions out of thoughtful, mature responses to their children's feelings and concerns, parents who, balancing their children's wishes with the parents' adult experience, decide what boundaries would best enable their children to explore the world, to learn and grow, while still being safe and learning to respect the rights of others. I have seen people who were able to affect children by having first been actively affected by those children with love, compassion, patience, and imagination.

I have seen people who loved children enough to realize that mere unilateral obedience is the least of virtues, valuable for preventing children from running out in front of trucks but with little use for understanding or nurturing children's hopes, dreams, and creative abilities. Merely demanding obedience gives adults little power to teach children to think for themselves, to make their own decisions, develop their own values or creativity, or grow in mutually loving relationships with their parents and others.

Parenting that exercises relational power is hard work. It takes a lot of patience, self-control, emotional strength, and a willingness to bear much of the price for the children's mistakes. But the reward for relational parenting is a greater joy at children's accomplishments, and a deeper, more mutual love as children develop their own relational power.

Bernard Loomer was clear that inequality of power will always be with us since obviously people differ in economic, political, and physical power. In addition to these differences, Loomer contends: "We differ in energy, ambition, intelligence, emotional intensity, relational sensitivity, imagination, creativity, addiction to evil and other forms of destructiveness, and the capacity to love. We are strikingly unequal in power, in our capacity to influence others for good or ill, by fair means or foul."[2] In a unilateral model, the burdens of inequality are borne most heavily by those who are weaker: "The natural and inevitable inequalities among individuals and groups become the means whereby the estrangements in life become wider and deeper. The rich become richer, and the poor become poorer. The strong become stronger and the weak become weaker and more dependent."[3]

Loomer emphasizes that there is a price to be paid even for those with great unilateral strength, for their strength lies in impoverishing their own relationships. They must learn not to care about the sufferings of others.

> The world of the individual who can be influenced by another without losing his or her identity or freedom is larger than the world of the individual who fears being influenced. The former can include ranges and depths of complexity and contrast to a degree that is not possible for the latter. The stature of the individual who can let another exist in her or his own creative freedom is larger than the size of the individual who insists that others must conform to his own purposes and understandings.[4]

Faced with inevitable inequalities, people with relational power will choose to bear a larger burden so that the weaker have a chance to develop their own relational power. Unlike unilateral power, relational power is not competitive in the sense of being mutually exclusive. Relational power is like love: The more we love each other, the more both of us can grow in love. To achieve this state will require that we take turns carrying the burden of love when one of us is less loving, but, in the long run, your goal is to increase my love, my relational power, and for me to increase yours. As Loomer explains, "In the life of relational power, the unfairness means that those of larger size must undergo greater suffering and bear a greater burden in sustaining those relationships that hopefully may heal the brokenness of the seamless web of interdependence in which we all live."[5]

People who live in relational power discover values to which they would otherwise have been blind. By listening with active openness, they help other people to articulate their own values more clearly and so to bring a richer vision of value into the relationship. "Under the relational conception of power, what is truly for the good of anyone or all of the relational partners is not a preconceived good. The true good is not a function of controlling or dominating influence. The true good is an emergent from deeply mutual relationships."[6]

Powerful examples of this are evident in the last fifty years as women, people of "color,"[7] cultural minorities, and people with diverse sexual orientations have been able to enrich our cultural conversation and political arena with a deeper sensitivity to the positive values they offer, as well as a greater awareness of the oppressive character of many of our cultural assumptions and practices.

Just as Gandhi insisted that there was nothing passive about nonviolence (*ahimsa*), Loomer emphasizes that relational power is different from passivity or unilateral weakness. Relational power does not mean letting other people control or manipulate you. As I suggested above, relational power has three vital elements: (1) the ability to be actively open to and affected by the world around us; (2) the ability to create ourselves out of what we have taken in; and (3) the ability to influence those about us by having first been affected by them. So, as you actively listen to the concerns and values of others, you also bring your own best judgment to bear in deciding who you will be in this relationship, what you want to contribute out of your own wisdom, how you want to change yourself and your values in the face of new experiences, and what you want to contribute to the relationship that may shape others involved. There is nothing weak or passive in such self-creativity. It requires enormous strength. This is never truer than when the contrasts between your values and the other person's values are greatest.

Ultimately, growth in relational power takes us beyond the human community. A process-relational vision of the world makes it clear that we humans are not the only members of the world community to experience pain or pleasure or values of our own. We are inescapably part of the larger ecological web that supports us, sustains us, and enriches our lives with beauty. It may take even greater relational power to become open to the values experienced by those nonhuman members of our community, but in the long run, we must develop the power to perceive those values, or we will surely continue to do massive damage to the ecological web essential to our own survival.[8]

We are so trapped in political, economic, and social structures of unilateral power that it often seems foolishly idealistic to take love and relational power seriously as models for life and social change. Yet, the Buddha, Gandhi, Jesus, and Martin Luther King Jr. are obvious public examples of great relational power. They lived out of a relational vision. (Indeed, King wrote his doctoral dissertation on a process theologian, Henry Nelson Wieman, who explicitly articulated a relational approach to life and creative transformation.) In my lifetime, I have seen my culture genuinely struggle to listen to the voices of women, minorities, and even children. We have made some strides toward changing our models of parenting. Violence toward children, women, "people of color," and others, while still all too common, is no longer seen as normal or acceptable. All of these groups have at least begun to have some genuine voice in our culture, despite powerful forces wanting to retain a culture of unilateral control.

A relational vision of reality may assist us in articulating more clearly and effectively a relational vision of power, in which power and love are two faces of the same strength, enriching all our lives.

John B. Cobb Jr. and others have approached the issue of power from a somewhat different direction. They emphasize the contrast between coercion and persuasion. Most of the world acts coercively. An individual electron has some tiny capacity for self-creativity, but by and large it is subject to the coercive power of past actualities. As organisms become more complex and more relationally sensitive to their environment, the range of possibilities they confront increases. To some extent persuasion, like relational power, goes all the way down, as we will see in the next chapter. But openness to persuasion as we usually think of it arises only with consciousness, only with the ability to conceptualize alternative futures, to envision a world other than the one actualized so far.

In human relationships, Cobb observes, the difference between coercion and persuasion is the difference between relationships that diminish freedom and those that increase it:

> The role of parent and teacher, in my view, is primarily to add to the range within which children can choose by calling attention to relevant propositions that are lures for feeling. Children thereby have their range of choice expanded without having the decision among the propositions decided for them. . . . Unilateral power is exercised coercively to whatever extent it limits the freedom of the receiver. It is exercised persuasively to whatever extent it increases the freedom of the recipient.[9]

Just as Loomer argued that it takes greater strength to be Jesus, Gandhi, or Martin Luther King Jr. than to be a dictator, Cobb would remind us that there is much greater power in the ability to change the hearts and minds of people through persuasion than to simply order them about or kill them.

LOOKING AHEAD

What would perfect, infinite, relational, and persuasive power be like? In a relational vision, what makes freedom possible? These questions bring us to the basic concepts of creativity and freedom, to Whitehead's vision of God, and to our next flight of imaginative exploration.

Creativity, Freedom, and God 9

WHAT MAKES FREEDOM POSSIBLE?

God is the great companion—the fellow-sufferer who understands.
—Alfred North Whitehead, *Process and Reality*

THE HIGHER our airplane of imaginative generalization and vision flies, the more crucial it is that we check our imagination by landing on the ground of "widespread, recurrent experience" and also that we remember Whitehead's opening admonitions.

> There remains the final reflection, how shallow, puny, and imperfect are efforts to sound the depths in the nature of things. In philosophical discussion, the merest hint of dogmatic certainty as to finality of statement is an exhibition of folly. (*PR* xiv)

> Rationalism never shakes off its status of an experimental adventure. . . . Rationalism is an adventure in the clarification of thought, progressive and never final. But it is an adventure in which even partial success has importance. (*PR* 9)

CREATIVITY

Everything that is actual becomes and perishes. Becoming is the ultimate fact underlying all others. How can we speak of "becoming"? It is not any particular thing or kind of thing. We can never point at becoming apart from specific events that become. Yet it is a feature shared by all things. Whitehead refers to this ultimate fact, this ultimate character shared by all actual things, as creativity. Although artistic or intellectual creativity would be instances of it, they are far too specific for our purpose here. We refer only to this fundamental fact that things become and perish.

> "Creativity" is the universal of universals characterizing ultimate matter of fact. It is that ultimate principle by which the many, which are the universe disjunctively, become the one actual occasion, which is the universe conjunctively. It lies in the nature of things that the many enter into complex unity. "Creativity" is the principle of novelty. (*PR* 21)

Creativity is not a mysterious power *behind* the world that makes it go. It is not fate, destiny, or a power that works for either good or evil. Creativity is simply the ultimate feature shared by all that is actual—God and the world alike.

FREEDOM

Whitehead described creativity as "the principle of novelty (*PR* 21) and attested that "[t]he universe is thus a creative advance into novelty" (*PR* 222). In one sense, this novelty is simply the emergence into existence of new events that have never existed before. In each moment of your awareness, you have a novel moment of experience that you have never had before. You may have had many kisses, but each one is different from the ones before, and you will never have your first kiss back again. Novelty inescapably involves perishing.

Whitehead also saw novelty as inherently involving freedom. Here you must remember what was said in chapter 4 about rocks. Rocks are not individuals, so they probably have no individual experience and no freedom. However, rocks are composed, ultimately, of electrons, protons, and neutrons that are individuals. The Heisenberg uncertainty principle, which has been tested many times in modern physics and which is basic to quantum mechanics, asserts among other things that no matter what conditions we impose on an electron or any other elementary particle, we cannot know exactly what it will do. This is not simply because we are missing available information. One reason that we cannot know what it will do is that it apparently has more than one possible response to the conditions imposed on it.

It appears that an electron, in each moment of its existence, confronts a range of possibilities for its own becoming, constrained but not totally determined by the world around it. Confronted with two slits in a screen, it can "decide" which path to take. "The word 'decision' does not here imply conscious judgment, although in some 'decisions' consciousness will be a factor. The word is used in its root sense of a 'cutting off,'" Whitehead notes (*PR* 43). In other words, when an electron or other individual entity has two mutually exclusive possibilities before it, it must "cut off" one and choose the other. Or, perhaps more accurately, it must choose to actualize *this* range of possibilities and not *that* range of possibilities. By human standards, these decisions are incredibly trivial. Nonetheless, they happen. However far the determining causal forces of the universe push to constrain a decision of any individual, there is always some range of possibilities open to it for its own self-creativity, by which it puts its own stamp on the world (*PR* 47).

As these simple elementary units of existence are joined together to form more complex organisms, at least in those organisms we call "living," they seem to create a degree of unity that allows for more complex reactions to the environment. While the conditions that make such interactions possible will have biological descriptions, the more we know the clearer it becomes that "there is no absolute gap between 'living' and 'non-living' societies" (*PR* 102). The primary meaning of life is the capacity for novel reactions because life is essentially "a bid for freedom" (*PR* 104).

In human beings, this capacity for novelty becomes morally important. It becomes what we usually mean by freedom. "In the case of those actualities whose immediate experience is most completely open to us, namely, human beings, [our own experience of self-creativity] is the foundation of our experience of responsibility. . . . of self-approval or self-reproach, of freedom, of emphasis. This element in experience is too large to be put aside merely as misconstruction. It governs the whole tone of human life" (*PR* 47).

Our experience of freedom is another instance of what David Griffin calls "hard-core" common sense. At an intellectual level, a great many people have believed and do believe that we have no freedom—that our lives are entirely determined by God and/or by the causal forces of nature. I fully agree with Griffin that no one could act on or hold this belief at a deep level. You will have to land the airplane of our imaginative flight and check the facts of your own experience.

Do you find yourself in each moment confronting a range of possibilities for your becoming between which you must choose? What would it mean to live and act as if you were totally determined, as if you had no decisions to make, no freedom to exercise? I don't think any of us can even imagine it because we never experience such a state.

Let me be clear that the term *freedom* here does not mean simply "doing what I want to do." We can't always do what we want to do. But more importantly, freedom as "doing what I want to do" is quite compatible with total determinism—whether by God or nature. In the New Testament book Philippians (2:12–13), readers are told to "work out your own salvation with fear and trembling" but also that "God is at work in you, both to will and to work for his good pleasure." Many Christian theologians have taken this latter statement to mean that God may predestine us both to want to sin and to commit sin. We sin because we want to sin and thus sin "freely." But this sense of freedom is entirely compatible with God's having caused both the desire and the action. That is not the sense of freedom process thinkers affirm.

It is certainly true that we constantly experience ourselves as coerced and constrained by our circumstances, by the world and the people around us, by the limits of our own bodies, and especially by the reality of our past decisions. We can never escape these constraints. The past is done and can never be changed, and we create ourselves out of that past. Sometimes the options open to us seem trivial, and sometimes they may all seem bad. But we never find ourselves truly with only one option. We must always decide, whether we want to or not. Sometimes we love freedom; sometimes we hate it. But we can never escape it.

Remember Plato's teaching that "the definition of being is simply power," quoted in chapter 7. Charles Hartshorne, a founding figure in process philosophy, asserted that "*to be is to create....*" "Each experience is thus a free act, in its final unity a 'self-created' actuality. ..." "In short, *freedom is self-creation.*"[1] In this deep sense, freedom is absolutely inherent in actuality. No individual can exist without some act of decision as to its own becoming. If that is true, as process-relational thinkers believe it is, then even an omnipotent God could not have created an actual world devoid of freedom. In some degree, to be actual is to be free.[2]

GOD

Whitehead believed that God, far from controlling the world, is the very source of the world's freedom. "Apart from God, there could be no relevant novelty" (*PR* 164).

As a community of creative thinkers seeking novelty of insight, process-relational thinkers disagree on many aspects of process thought. Perhaps the most significant disagreements relate to the question of God. I am among those who think that Whitehead may have flown too high and reached too far beyond the ground of empirical justification when he felt that his vision of reality required the existence of a divine entity. Nevertheless, his reasons command respect. Furthermore, there is no denying that process thought has been more warmly received in theological circles than in departments of philosophy. This is partly because of the powerful antimetaphysical bias of much twentieth-century philosophy but also because the process-relational vision of God has spoken powerfully to many people and has enabled them to respond in creative and religiously important ways to a wide range of profound theological issues ranging from the relationship between science and religion, to the emerging voices of women, to the ancient problem of evil. In any case, we cannot understand Whitehead's vision without some introduction to his concept of God.

Although Whitehead became an atheist early in his career, over time he became convinced that the universe as he understood it could not function without the interaction of something he could only call God. A good analogy might be the discovery of the planet Neptune. Astronomers could not account for the paths of the outer planets.

Given what was known about the solar system, those planets should be following different orbits. Finally, after years of careful calculations, it was proposed that those orbits could best be accounted for by the presence of another planet with a specific mass moving in a specific orbit of its own. Once they knew what to look for and where to look, the astronomers found the new planet.

Whitehead offered a similar argument for God. With his typical bold humility, he acknowledged that "[t]here is nothing here in the nature of proof. There is merely the confrontation of the theoretic system with a certain rendering of the facts" (*PR* 343). He offered a broad vision of reality and suggested that the whole thing would make more sense and that our own immediate experience would be more adequately accounted for, if we include in that vision a specific concept of God. Why?

One of the most fundamental principles of life and philosophy is that you can't get something from nothing—the "ontological principle." Ever since Aristotle, it has been recognized that potentiality—possibilities—must be grounded in what is actual. No matter how much gunpowder or firewood you have as potential heat, there will be no explosion or fire without some actual heat. By the same token, there can be no freedom without a range of possibilities awaiting our decision. Those possibilities must be rooted in something actual.

Living after Charles Darwin, Whitehead was keenly aware that genuine novelty emerges in this world. Aristotle might have believed that every possibility had already been actualized, that every animal that would ever exist already existed, but Whitehead could not. He knew that this world had seen the emergence of many species of animals—including humans—and the emergence of these new forms required explanation. Also, of course, there is the persistent experience of possibilities in our own lives between which we must choose. If there have been and still are possibilities for becoming beyond those already actualized in the world, in what actuality can they reside? There seemed to Whitehead to be only one answer—God. But this is not a supernatural God who breaks all the rules and acts as a *deus ex machina*: "In the first place, God is not to be treated as an exception to all metaphysical principles, invoked to save their collapse. He is their chief exemplification" (*PR* 343).

Whitehead had no interest in a supernatural God. If God exists, God must be part of a comprehensive system of reality. And while God may be uniquely individual in some respects, God must also live by the same fundamental set of principles describing all that exists. There is to be no metaphysical cheating.

The fact of novelty and its attendant fact of freedom had pointed to a need for divine interaction with the world. It seemed to Whitehead that God was the only actuality in which all possibilities could reside, including those not yet actualized in the world.

Every event in the world, every momentary drop of experience, begins with a two-fold experience of God and the past actual world. It must create itself out of these relationships. Jointly, God and the world establish what must be, the facts that cannot be ignored, the raw material from which existence will be created. They also, jointly, provide each new drop of experience with the possibilities for its becoming. Whitehead was convinced that, if there were only the world, there could be no *new* possibilities, nothing that had not already been done. If that were the case, the world could only repeat itself. There must be something actual, in addition to the past world, that acts as the source of genuine novelty. Thus, "[a]part from the intervention of God, there could be nothing new in the world, and no order in the world. The course of creation would be a dead level of ineffectiveness, with all balance and intensity progressively excluded by the cross currents of incompatibility" (*PR* 247).

If all possibilities are to somehow reside in God, God must experience them. God must have experienced them forever, primordially. This eternal "envisagement" of all possibilities is what Whitehead called the "primordial nature of God" (*PR* 46, 343–51).

In some respects, the primordial nature of God has no moral character; it just is. The possibilities for the world are both good and bad: "This function of God is analogous to the remorseless working of things in Greek and in Buddhist thought. The initial aim is the best for that impasse. But if the best be bad, then the ruthlessness of God can be personified as Até, the goddess of mischief" (*PR* 244).

But this is not all there is to the story. John B. Cobb Jr.'s emphasis on persuasive power can now be appreciated more fully. Power is coercive as it works to constrain freedom by narrowing the possibilities before us. Power is persuasive as it tends to nurture freedom by opening up a wider range of novelty for our reactions to life. God's work in the world is inherently persuasive because, in every situation, God is the ground of novelty. God makes available and draws us toward a range of possibilities that enable us to envision a world beyond the world already actualized, to choose forms of self-creativity beyond what the world alone made possible. If "life" is defined in terms of a capacity for novelty, God's persuasive work in the world is the indispensable ground of life itself. Finally, God's persuasive work in us enables us to perceive visions of truth, beauty, and goodness that inspire the metaphor of a spark of divinity within every person:

> The sheer force of things lies in the intermediate physical process: this is the energy of physical production. God's role is not the combat of productive force with productive force, of destructive force with destructive force; it lies in the patient operation of the overpowering rationality of his conceptual harmonization. He does not create the world, he saves it: or, more accurately, he is the poet of the world, with tender patience leading it by his vision of truth, beauty, and goodness. (*PR* 464)

While it is helpful in some ways for Whitehead to distinguish between the primordial and consequent natures of God, ultimately these are only faces of a single reality. God is one, and, taken as a whole, God is decidedly moral. Here we must return to the concept of relational power.

GOD AND BECOMING

In Whitehead's world, God is part of the relational process. Not only does every drop of becoming experience God, but God experiences every drop of becoming. Thus, God also has a "consequent nature," which is God's infinitely complex experience of every single moment of becoming constituting the actual world—forever. God is good because God shares the experience of every creature—every pain, joy, hope, despair, failure, and triumph. God is not an *im*partial, *dis*interested observer of the world but the uniquely "*omni*-partial" and *totally* interested participant in every relationship there is. God knows what it is like to be you and me and "them" and the animals and plants we all eat. In the fullest sense possible, then, God is love: God is perfect relational power.

It is vital to emphasize again and again that God's power is *not* omnipotent unilateral or coercive power. Quite the opposite. God *cannot* coerce any creature. Every creature has its own freedom. Rather God is the persuasive ground of freedom. So God knows what we may choose and are likely to choose, but not what we will choose. God is omniscient (all knowing) in the sense that God knows everything there is to know, but since the future does not exist it is not there to be known. Only the possibilities for the future can be known perfectly. Nor can God remain unaffected by the world: God is the only one who has the strength, the ability, to be open to every single experience in the world. God is the only one who can take every thing in, integrate it with God's own infinitely ancient wisdom, and create God's self out of that relationship in each moment. God is the only one who can then feed back to every creature in the world a lure and call toward those possibilities that are best for it. All the possibilities are there, good and bad, but they come to us, Whitehead says, with God's call toward the better. Here, Whitehead waxes understandably poetic, and I can best quote at length:

> The consequent nature of God is his judgment on the world. He saves the world as it passes into the immediacy of his own life. It is the judgment of a tenderness which loses nothing that can be saved. It is also the judgment of a wisdom which uses what in the temporal world is mere wreckage. (*PR* 346)

> Another image which is also required to understand his consequent nature is that of his infinite patience. (*PR* 346)

> By reason of this reciprocal relation, the love in the world passes into the love in heaven, and floods back again into the world. In this sense, God is the great companion—the fellow-sufferer who understands. (*PR* 351)

> In this way the insistent craving is justified—the insistent

> craving that zest for existence be refreshed by the ever-present, unfading importance of our immediate actions, which perish and yet live for evermore. (*PR* 351)

SO WHAT?

There is so much more to be said about the process-relational vision of God. Under Whitehead's inspiration, process-relational theologians have felt encouraged to move beyond his preliminary insights to explore religious questions and problems in a whole array of new ways. A God who cannot control the world but who can suffer with us and draw us forward in love is a God who offers radically new responses to the ancient cry of human suffering.

Furthermore, a metaphysical vision that actively seeks to integrate itself with our knowledge from all sciences calls for a kind of theological discourse that makes theology open to being both challenged and enriched by everything we know and everything we learn. Process-relational theologians reject the idea of faith as mere "belief without evidence" in favor of faith as fidelity to the open-ended search for what is true and good, a search that at its best engages us continually in a relational process.

Looking Ahead 10

THE FUTURE OF PROCESS-RELATIONAL THOUGHT

Exemplary persons who study the way love others.
—CONFUCIUS, *THE ANALECTS*

IN THE INTRODUCTION to their translation of *The Analects of Confucius*, Roger T. Ames and Henry Rosemont Jr. describe the *substance* view of reality dominant in Western thought and languages, and sharply contrast it with an *event* view of reality reflected in Chinese language and thought. In the West we know that our experience reveals a world of constant change—the world of appearance—but we have claimed that our reason gives us access to an unchanging reality underneath all the change. Hence we have been obsessed by a split between appearance and reality. In contrast, Ames and Rosemont argue, we find "no discussion of underlying reality versus changing appearances in early Chinese texts: reality and appearance are one and the same, and the reality is that everything changes."[1]

> [E]arly Chinese thinkers never seem to have perceived any substances that remained the *same* through time; rather in our interpretation they saw "things" relationally, and related differently, at different periods of time. *Dao*, the totality of all things . . . is a process that requires the language of both "change" . . . and "persistence" . . . to captures its dynamic disposition.[2]

Rosemont and Ames interpret the Tao (the Way) in equally process-relational terms. "'The way' is defined as 'treading,'" as the *Zhuangzi* says, "The way is made in the walking of it."[3]

It is not surprising, then, that as I write in the spring of 2007, there are seventeen centers for process-relational thought open in China, and two more scheduled to open this summer along with the second Process Summer Academy in China. There have already been several conferences on process thought and various aspects of constructive postmodernism in China related to education, the economy, and the environment. An International Whitehead conference is scheduled in Bangalore, India, and other process-relational conferences and centers have been created in countries around the world. Process-relational theology also has a significant voice in religious communities around the globe.

Of course, these gentle voices are difficult to hear in a world raging with war, injustice, poverty, and religious strife. Process-relational thinking is more likely to "dwell upon the tender elements in the world, which slowly and in quietness operate by love" (*PR* 343).

It is too easy to say that a world rooted in process-relational thinking would spring forth in love and justice. We could say the same about the teachings of the Buddha, Jesus, and others. Nevertheless, I would be this bold. In the process-relational vision we are once again invited, beckoned, to see and to *feel*, what we have been called to see and feel by other great visions of life—our personal relatedness to all creatures and the moral obligations and challenges that that relatedness calls forth. We are called to care for the common good, to work intelligently and lovingly for social and economic justice, sustainable economic and environmental practices, religious teachings and practices that nurture harmony rather than hatred, and political structures that empower rather than coerce and impoverish.

This little book has merely introduced you to the philosophical vision underlying the efforts of process thinkers to work for the common good. We hope that other volumes will follow that explore the concrete connections and applications of process-relational thinking to economics, the environment, politics, religion, Asian traditions, ethics, education, and more. We may hope against all hope that the twenty-first century will find us becoming, slowly, more deeply relational, wise, and compassionate. Since I quoted the Hindu Bhagavad Gita unfavorably in chapter 5, let me make amends here by concluding with my favorite passages from the Gita (edited for inclusive language), verses with a beautiful vision of ethical relationships beckoning us toward process-relational compassion.

Their every action
Is wed to the welfare
Of other creatures.[4]
Those who burn with the bliss
And suffer the sorrow
Of every creature
Within their own hearts,
Making their own
Each bliss and each sorrow:
Them I hold highest.[5]

ACTUAL ENTITIES (ALSO ACTUAL OCCASIONS)

Everything is in process, becoming and perishing. But what kind of reality can become and perish? Events. The smallest events are momentary drops of experience or *feeling*. These are the building blocks of reality. Your mind, your flow of awareness, for example, is a series of such events. So, perhaps, is an electron or some smaller component of which an electron is composed. Your mind, and also any of the smallest units of existence like electrons or quarks, is a series of what Whitehead called "actual entities" or "actual occasions." An actual entity is a drop or event of space-time; it is a drop of feeling. You experience the feelings of previous moments in your life, especially, but not exclusively, the most recent ones. You also react to the feelings of the actual entities composing your body. An electron feels the spatial-temporal feelings of other actual occasions, and these physical feelings constitute the physical structure of the universe that physicists describe in other language. The universe is a vast web or field of microevents. "[T]he actual world is a process, and the process is the becoming of actual entities" (*PR* 22).

> "Actual entities"—also termed "actual occasions"—are the final real things of which the world is made up. There is no going behind actual entities to find anything more real. They differ among themselves: God is an actual entity, and so is the most trivial puff of existence in far-off empty space. But, though there are gradations of importance, and diversities of function, yet in the principles which actuality exemplifies all are on the same level. The final facts are, all alike, actual entities; and these actual entities are drops of experience, complex and interdependent (*PR* 18).

I have long thought that Whitehead was a little careless here when he spoke of actual entities "in" space. He should have said "constituting" empty space. Whitehead meant to help us see that space itself is composed of events, of actual entities and their relationships.[3] As modern physicists teach us, space is not an empty vessel within which things happen. We call space "empty" when it is not being occupied by enduring physical objects, but space itself is a web of events and relationships. That is why physicists say that the big bang did not happen "in space." The big bang was itself the creation of the space of the universe, and that space is continuing to expand. The whole universe of space, energy, mass, and time is one vast network of events—of actual entities. Similarly, your personal experience does not happen "in" your mind; your mind simply *is* the flow of your experience. That flow, in Whitehead's language, is a series of actual entities or actual occasions.

If Becoming is a series of events, why do we experience it as a continuous flow? The answer is that there is nothing between events, no time between the drops of time.[4] A helpful but risky analogy might be to think of watching a movie projected from an old-fashioned reel of film. Although the movie is composed of a series of individual frames, we see it as a flow. Despite this, the movie image is misleading in two crucial ways. First, the movie is more like the traditional Christian view of time in which the future already exists, just waiting for us to view it. In that view, there can be no freedom since our decisions in future frames have already been made by us. In the process model, each new frame is coming into existence, determined by its past and its own self-creative freedom. The second vital difference is that, in process-relational philosophy, that self-creative act is relational. The frames do not just sit there in atomic isolation. No actual entity is atomic in Descartes' sense that a substance exists independently. Each new moment must create itself out of the previous world. The past is the material for the self-creative action of the present moments. Then the cycle happens all over again.

Actual entities become and perish. Change is the difference between these events.

> [T]he notion of an actual entity as the unchanging subject of change is completely abandoned. . . . The ancient doctrine that "no one crosses the same river twice" is extended. No thinker thinks twice; and, to put the matter more generally, no subject experiences twice. (*PR* 29)

An actual entity is an expression of what physicists mean when they speak of quantum events. I recall an old animated science video attempting to explain quantum events by the difference between milk pouring continuously from a pitcher and milk coming in quart cartons. Both may come at the rate of one gallon per second, but the cartons come as quantum units. Either you get a whole quart, or you get none at all, although this image, too, fails us, since it suggests that the quarts are isolated from each other. This isn't the place to defend quantum physics, and no doubt unanswered questions will remain in many readers' minds, but it may help that what Whitehead is proposing is simply another view of what quantum physics experimentally demonstrates—energy comes as packets. Whitehead quoted William James as saying:

> Either your experience is of no content, of no change, or it is of a perceptible amount of content or change. Your acquaintance with reality grows literally by buds or drops of perception. Intellectually and on reflection you can divide these into components, but as immediately given, they come totally or not at all. (*PR* 68)

Here are a few more key passages from Whitehead's *Process and Reality* that may help give some picture of actual entities. In each case, the best model for understanding actual entities, I think, is the series of moments constituting the flow of your own experience.

> [T]he actual world is built up of actual occasions and by the ontological principle whatever things there are in any sense of "existence" are derived by abstraction from actual occasions.... An actual occasion is the limiting type of an event with only one member. (*PR* 73)

> [H]ow an actual entity becomes constitutes what that actual entity is;... Its "being" is constituted by its "becoming." This is the principle of process. (*PR* 23)

> An entity is actual, when it has significance for itself. (*PR* 25)

ETERNAL OBJECTS

At least since Plato and Aristotle, Western philosophers have distinguished between what is actual and what is possible or potential. The qualities "circleness" and "blueness" might be seen as general possibilities that are made more or less actual in a particular round or blue thing. In the philosophic tradition, they are often referred to as universals, to indicate that many different particular things may be round or blue. Following Plato's tradition, Whitehead saw these possibilities as themselves never changing. Consequently, he called them "eternal objects." The word *eternal* has no religious or honorific implications. We might say that they are nontemporal; hence, by themselves they are not actual. They depend upon actualization by particular actual entities. An "eternal object" is a "pure potential," according to Whitehead (*PR* 23).

As explained in chapter 9, God's "envisagement" of the eternal objects forms is God's primordial nature. God's consequent nature is God's prehension of the actual entities constituting the world. Remember, of course, that God is one. So these are merely conceptual distinctions Whitehead used to explore aspects of the divine experience and function. In that sense, Whitehead suggested that the primordial nature does not change since eternal objects don't change. What is possible in the broadest sense is always possible. But since the world is constantly becoming, God's consequent nature is constantly acquiring new experience. For example, 2 + 2 = 4 is always true, and God has always known it. But every time a child learns this for the first time, it is that child's first time, and it is the first time God has ever experienced that child learning it. In the divine life, the primordial and the new are woven together into God's creative response to the creative advance of the world.

PREHENSIONS: PHYSICAL, CONCEPTUAL, HYBRID

Each actual entity must create itself out of the past actualities. It must take that past into itself. Metaphorically, we might say that it must reach out and grasp those past actual entities, draw them in, and create itself out of them. Whitehead appeals to our use of the term *apprehend*, as when the police apprehend or "grasp" a criminal. So Whitehead says that an actual entity "prehends" previous actual entities.

At the conscious level, memory would be prehension. We experience a past experience again, but we do it from the current perspective. We feel past feelings. One student of mine illustrated this by relating that, as a kindergartener, she had once wet her pants in class. Sometimes, she reports, she still feels a return rush of embarrassment when she recalls the event. Feelings carry emotional tone.

Physical prehension is the feeling of a past actual entity. *Conceptual prehension* is the feeling of an eternal object—a possibility. However, since possibilities must always reside in some actuality—in God if nowhere else—and since every actual entity must actualize some possibilities, it would be fair to say that we never can have a purely physical or conceptual prehension. *Hybrid prehension* means jointly feeling an actual entity and an eternal object. The distinction between physical and conceptual prehensions is a matter of analysis, of understanding the different dimensions of all experience. Also, the dominance of physical and conceptual changes. When I put a spoonful of hot fudge sauce in my mouth, I usually just focus on the sheer physical pleasure, but at some level that pleasure carries the lure toward the possibility of taking another spoonful. Conversely, as I sit at my computer and think of our next visit to our new grandson, that imaginative look toward the future is inescapably felt in conjunction with our previous visits and the felt pleasures of hearing his laugh and the smell of poopy diapers.

Positive prehension suggests actively taking into oneself the experiences of the past as material for self-creativity. It means feeling the feelings of previous moments—as when you feel the emotion you felt just a moment ago or when a photon feels the physical causal force of previous events.

Obviously, there must be a selecting out, as well. We can actualize only some possibilities. We can use only some of the experiences of the past in the present moment. The whole past is there. If the big bang had never occurred, you and I would not be here. It plays some role in the history out of which we must create ourselves. Yet, we cannot incorporate every aspect of the infinite past because we are finite creatures. Only God could positively prehend infinity.

Every past actual entity must be prehended and dealt with in some way, but that prehension is selective. *Negative prehension* means blocking out those elements of past actual entities that will not be incorporated into the present moment. Still, even what we block out has an impact on us. Psychotherapists often work to help people understand how they are affected by what they do *not* remember consciously, and we know the impact can be very great.

> In this process, the negative prehensions which effect the elimination are not merely negligible. . . . The negative prehensions have their own subjective forms which they contribute to the process. A feeling bears on itself the scars of its birth; it recollects as a subjective emotion its struggle for existence; it retains the impress of what it might have been, but is not. It is for this reason that what an actual entity has avoided as a datum for feeling may yet be an important part of its equipment. The actual cannot be reduced to mere matter of fact divorced from the potential. (*PR* 226–27)

DIPOLAR (OR BIPOLAR) EXPERIENCE

"Every instance of experience is dipolar, whether that instance be God or an actual occasion of the world" (*PR* 36). *Dipolar* means that its experience has both physical and conceptual/mental aspects. Remember that *conceptual* and *mental* are technical terms here that do not presuppose consciousness or thought. Every event is "physical" in the sense that it arises out of the stubborn facts of the past world and is "mental" or "conceptual" in the sense that it must confront, decide between, and actualize a range of possibilities for its own becoming. Thus, every actual entity has a *physical pole* and a *mental pole*, though these are fully integrated into one complex experience.

One meaning of this is that there is no ultimate dualism between mind and body. Ultimately, there are not two kinds of distinct realities—physical and mental—as Descartes believed. There is only one ultimate kind of reality that involves both the physical and the mental. In the most basic respects, they are all alike, while in others they differ importantly.

Most actual entities in the universe are dominated by their physical pole—by their experience of spatial-temporal causal relations. Yet even the simplest of events constituting the spatial-temporal world around us must also experience those eternal objects—those possibilities—relevant to their own becoming. To this trivial extent, they have a conceptual or mental pole and some freedom.

In your own experience, there is always a physical dimension because your mind arises out of the physical activity of your body, especially your brain. But your mind obviously has an important mental pole as well. Sometimes the conceptual almost totally overwhelms the physical, as when you are deeply absorbed in thinking about a particular problem. More often the reverse is true.

The difference between the actual entities constituting the flow of your mind and those composing the physical world is one of degree, not kind. Put another way, being dipolar means that each actual entity involves both the experience of the past world and the possibilities for its own becoming as contributing to a possible future.

CONCRESCENCE

Concrescence is an actual entity's process of becoming concrete. It means sorting out the many things that might be and settling on what will be. Finally, each actual entity must become "this" rather than "that," however complex "this" may be. The new actual entity confronts the whole past actual world, rich with causal power and possibilities, and brings that world together into one new entity, a novel event.

> The "production of novel togetherness" is the ultimate notion embodied in the term "concrescence." (*PR* 21)

> "Concrescence" is the name for the process in which the universe of many things acquires an individual unity. . . . There are not "the concrescence" and "the novel thing": when we analyse the novel thing we find nothing but the concrescence. "Actuality" means nothing else than this ultimate entry into the concrete. . . . (*PR* 211)

Principle of Relativity

Everything is related to everything else. Everything that has ever happened in the past has some impact on the present. Everything that happens in the present has some impact on events in the future.[5]

> [I]t belongs to the nature of a "being" that it is a potential for every "becoming." This is the "principle of relativity." (*PR* 22)

> The principle of universal relativity directly traverses [contradicts] Aristotle's dictum "A substance is not present in a subject." On the contrary, according to this principle an actual entity is present in other actual entities. In fact if we allow for degrees of relevance and for negligible relevance, we must say that every [past] actual entity is present in every other [future] actual entity. (*PR* 50)

INITIAL AIM AND SUBJECTIVE AIM

The discussion of initial and subjective aims brings us back to chapters 8 and 9, regarding relational power, causation, freedom, and God.

Each actual entity is a drop of experience with self-creativity. Self-creativity requires some aim, some goal. According to Whitehead, each actual entity begins with an "initial aim." Whitehead said, "Thus the initial stage of the aim is rooted in the nature of God, and its completion depends on the self-causation of the subject-superject" (that is, the actual entity) (*PR* 244).[6] The initial aim is the causal force of the past, combined with God's presentation of the relevant possibilities *and* a "lure" toward some rather than others. For most basic events, there is very little room for "decision." Even for humans, our range of options is often very small, and sometimes all the options seem bad.

> This function of God is analogous to the remorseless working of things in Greek and in Buddhist thought. The initial aim is the best for that impasse. But if the best be bad, then the ruthlessness of God can be personified as Até the goddess of mischief. (*PR* 244)

Whitehead observed that

> The secularization of the concept of God's functions in the world is at least as urgent a requisite of thought as is the

> secularization of other elements in experience. The concept of God is certainly an essential element in religious feelings. But the converse is not true; the concept of religious feeling is not an essential element in the concept of God's function in the universe. (*PR* 207)

Most experience of God is not what we usually think of as "religious"; it is simply the working out of the creative advance. Every actual entity, whether of a human mind or an electron, begins with an experience of the past world and also an experience of those possibilities relevant to its own becoming. Whitehead argued that the experience of novel possibilities (eternal objects) entails an experience of God.[7] Thus, every momentary event of every electron, quark, and human mind involves an experience of God. But for most of the universe, and for most of us most of the time, that would only mean the experience of those possibilities that help sustain the functional order of the cosmos and of our lives. Only rarely in human experience would our experience of God be of that character that people mean when they speak of religious experience, though Whitehead's vision has powerful religious implications and we can imagine a mystic, saint, or Buddhist monk learning to be conscious of the divine dimension of experience much more consistently than the rest of us.[8]

On reflection, we can easily see that most of the infinite range of possibilities is not relevant for any particular occasion. There might well be possibilities for a universe with seven spatial dimensions, but they cannot be actualized here. Indeed, having decided to sit at my desk and work, I have made irrelevant most of those possibilities relevant to my having been elsewhere at this moment. So, Whitehead distinguished between *pure potentialities* and *relevant possibilities* (or *real potentiality*) (*PR* 23). In this respect, God helps to provide order and stability in the world.

While the role of God is partly one of helping to create an ordered cosmos, it is also to generate novelty and to enable self-creativity. Hence, God's activity gives rise to the Heisenberg uncertainty principle in quantum physics, to life understood as the capacity for significantly novel responses to the world, to the possibility of bio logical novelty expressed in mutations and evolution, and to moral freedom in human beings. Whitehead argued that this capacity for novelty at every level is derived from God.

> Apart from God, there could be no relevant novelty. (*PR* 164)
>
> Apart from the intervention of God, there could be nothing new in the world, and no order in the world. The course of creation would be a dead level of ineffectiveness, with all balance and intensity progressively excluded by the cross currents of incompatibility. The novel hybrid feelings derived from God, with the derivative sympathetic conceptual valuations, are the foundations of progress. (*PR* 247)

Each actual entity "derives from God its basic conceptual aim, relevant to its actual world, yet with indeterminations awaiting its own decisions" (*PR* 244). Freedom, however, requires that the actual entity have the power to determine its *own* aim—its *subjective aim*—which may be different from God's aim. If we had no other choice than to follow God's aim, there would still be no freedom. So remember that the initial aim includes *all* of the possibilities relevant for the becoming of a particular actual entity—even if those possibilities include mass murder. However much God may seek to persuade us away from those terrible possibilities, Plato was right that "the definition of being is simply power,"[9] and every actual entity has the power to create itself within the limits provided by the actual world. The self-creativity includes the capacity to take what is given and create its own subjective aim.

Here, I think, we confront the paradox of freedom. How can an actual entity choose its own aim? Must it not have some aim by which it decides the aim by which it will decide? Do we not confront a "vicious regress" here that makes freedom impossible? The Protestant reformer Martin Luther appealed to this argument to insist that our will must finally be determined by either God or Satan, and we are simply like mules over which two riders battle.[10] We have nothing to say about it. Similarly, Gottfried Wilhelm Leibniz argued that every effect must have a sufficient cause.[11] This is basically another way to assert the ontological principle that you can't get something from nothing. No event can occur without a specific set of conditions. Those conditions are necessary. But if those conditions are all present, they become sufficient. Given those conditions, the event *must* occur. The arguments of Luther and Leibniz make the common point that events cannot be their own cause. Since only other events can bring them into existence, the world must be totally deterministic.

Freedom seems to require that there is an element of self-causation for which there is no sufficient reason beyond the choice of the chooser! This is exactly what Whitehead asserted when he wrote: "[I]n each concrescence whatever is determinable is determined, but that there is always a remainder for the decision of the subject-superject of that concrescence. . . . This final decision is the reaction of the unity of the whole to its own internal determination" (*PR* 27–28).

Any resolution of this paradox, if one is possible, requires far more examination than can be accomplished here. Speaking personally, I find the purely rational arguments against freedom to be powerful. As an empiricist, however, I have to say that knowledge of the world must always, finally, arise from experience. Ever since Galileo, experience has trumped theory when the two collide. I am persuaded by Whitehead that some element of freedom is an inescapable dimension of my experience. I certainly experience the powerful determining forces of the past, yet it is impossible for me to live or act without *presupposing* that I have choices to make.

Morally relevant freedom requires more than an aim for the immediate moment:

> The subjective aim, whereby there is origination of conceptual feelings, is at intensity of feeling (a) in the immediate subject, and (b) in the relevant future.
>
> This double aim—at the immediate present and the relevant future—is less divided than appears on the surface. For the determination of the relevant future, and the anticipatory feeling respecting provision for its grade of intensity,

> are elements affecting the immediate complex of feeling. The greater part of morality hinges on the determination of relevance in the future. The relevant future consists of those elements in the anticipated future which are felt with effective intensity by the present subject by reason of the real potentiality for them to be derived from itself. (*PR* 27)

This quotation describes my own experience so accurately that I cannot help but anticipate that it will speak to you as well. We constantly seek to balance, integrate, or sometimes battle between the pull of the present moment weighed against the needs of tomorrow. But the aim at tomorrow's needs is often precisely what creates satisfaction in the present. Anticipation of satisfaction for tomorrow's achievement feels good today.

SOCIETIES

Clearly, we cannot simply look around and see individual actual entities any more than we can look around and see individual electrons or quarks. The objects we see in the world would be examples of what Whitehead called *societies*. These range from the subatomic level to "crystals, rocks, planets, and suns" (*PR* 102) and also include living organisms.

Whitehead referred to his philosophy as a "philosophy of organism" and often expressed his ideas in social terms.[12] In both metaphors, he wanted to move away from the purely atomic and mechanistic models that dominated modern science through the nineteenth century and are still powerful today.

A society is a group of actual entities connected in specific ways. Mainly, they share certain "defining characteristics" in ways that enable the society to hang together (*PR* 89). A *structured society* has other societies within it. For example, your body is a structured society including many levels of *subordinate societies*—bodily organs, cells, molecules, atoms, etc. Societies that endure over time may be said to have *personal order*. Your mind would be an example of a society with a personal order but so would a molecule.

A society is also a *nexus*. *Nexus* is a broader term that can include any kind of togetherness of actual entities. "A non-social nexus is what answers to the notion of 'chaos'" (*PR* 72). Structured societies, like living cells, in whom novel responses to their environment have importance,

> are termed "living." It is obvious that a structured society may have more or less "life," and that there is no absolute gap between "living" and "non-living" societies. For certain purposes, whatever "life" there is in a society may be important; and for other purposes, unimportant. (*PR* 102)

It is important to realize, however, that Whitehead is not an old-fashioned "vitalist," thinking of "life" as some mysterious force, as when fantasy stories speak of having the "life force" sucked from a body. He means that actual occasions are "living" when they are dominated by novel responses to their environment rather than by the controlling forces of the past. Thus, Whitehead's approach to life was another rejection of supernaturalism and of Cartesian dualism. Life is part of nature, in us as much as in anything else, and the boundaries between organic and inorganic, living and nonliving, conscious and nonconscious are blurry. The universe is not basically dualistic, even here.

OBJECTIFICATION

An actual entity is a subject of its own experience. It is a self-creative drop of feeling. When an actual entity completes its process of becoming, "This final unity is termed the 'satisfaction'" (*PR* 212). It achieves its subjective aim. Whitehead also refers to this completed process—the actual entity that has become and now perishes—as a *subject-superject*. He uses this strange term to remind us that an actual entity is a drop of experience or feeling. While it becomes, it is a subject of its own feeling. Once it has become and perished, it becomes raw material to be prehended by future actual entities. What they prehend are its feelings. It is no longer a subject for itself, but its feelings will be felt by others. This is the point of the term *subject-superject*. The feelings of past events are felt in the present—with modifications by the present actual entities.

Whitehead also spoke of the *objectification* of the past by the present. What was a subject becomes an object. What was a moment of self-creativity becomes a fixed and unchangeable fact. Once again, reflect on your own experience. You face a decision. You confront possibilities and struggle between them. The process of reflection, decision, and action involves a long series of actual occasions constituting the flow of your mind. To see objectification most clearly, imagine that you have decided and acted, that these specific decisions and actions, however subjective at the moment, are now settled and done. Nothing can change them. All future occasions must deal with them as objective facts. There may be many ways in which later on you can confront, deny, rethink, reframe, try to undo the damage, or build on the success. But what was once a subjective decision must now be confronted as objective fact.

OBJECTIVE IMMORTALITY

Although Whitehead did not completely rule out the possibility of life after death, he was convinced that a mind (soul/psyche) is the flow of a body's experience, so he thought it unlikely that it could survive the death of its body. When the body can no longer sustain a unified flow of experience, that flow perishes. Consequently, there is probably no *subjective* immortality. However, every event has *objective* immortality in the sense that it becomes a fact of which the future must always take account.

There is a special sense of objective immortality in Whitehead's vision, and that is the way each actual entity is taken up into the life of God. God's consequent nature, as explained before, is God's ongoing experience of the becoming and perishing of the actual entities forming the world. The experience of each actual entity is prehended fully by God. In other words, God has infinite relational power. With regard to God's experience of the world, Whitehead wrote:

> In it there is no loss, no obstruction. The world is felt in a unison of immediacy. The property of combining creative advance with the retention of mutual immediacy is what in the previous section is meant by "everlasting."

> The wisdom of subjective aim prehends every actuality for what it can be in such a perfected system—its sufferings, its sorrows, its failures, its triumphs, its immediacies of joy—woven by rightness of feeling into the harmony of the universal feeling, which is always immediate, always many, always one, always with novel advance, moving onward and never perishing. The revolts of destructive evil, purely self-regarding, are dismissed into their triviality of merely individual facts; and yet the good they did achieve in individual joy, in individual sorrow, in the introduction of needed contrast, is yet saved by its relation to the completed whole. The image—and it is but an image—the image under which this operative growth of God's nature is best conceived, is that of a tender care that nothing be lost. (*PR* 346)

If we remember that what is taken into God's life is not the mere fact of our existence but the dynamic feelings of our life, then there is room for an interesting discussion about what this might mean. Also, John B. Cobb Jr. and David Ray Griffin have both given this matter significant attention and think there may be room for some forms of continued experience. While I am skeptical, I appreciate the fact that they urge us to step back, shake off preconceptions, use some imagination, examine all the evidence, and go with what the evidence and our best, most honest thinking supports.[13]

CONCLUSION

Let me end with a return to bold humility. As Plato confessed in the *Timaeus*, the most we can hope for is a likely tale. Whitehead concurs, as we have seen previously:

> There remains the final reflection, how shallow, puny, and imperfect are efforts to sound the depths in the nature of things. In philosophical discussion, the merest hint of dogmatic certainty as to finality of statement is an exhibition of folly. (*PR* xiv)

> Rationalism never shakes off its status of an experimental adventure. . . . Rationalism is an adventure in the clarification of thought, progressive and never final. But it is an adventure in which even partial success has importance. (*PR* 9)

The airplane continues to fly and land, fly and land. I invite you to continue the adventure.

Notes

Chapter 1: A Process-Relational World

1. Alfred North Whitehead, *Process and Reality*, ed. David Ray Griffin and Donald W. Sherburne, corr. ed. (New York: Free Press, 1978). *Process and Reality* was first published in 1929. All further references to this work will be cited in the text as *PR*.
2. From a conversation with my colleague, Dan Keegan.
3. More precisely, we might say that the future is not *actual*. There is a sense in which *possibilities* for the future do exist, but that is a distinction we don't need to worry about now. Also, to say that "the future does not exist" does *not* mean that there is a *specific* future (*the* future) already settled upon and waiting to exist. Rather there is a vast range of possibilities that might be actualized in the future, and the creative advance awaits the decisions of the present. The universe is a continuous series of self-creative events arising out of the past and confronting many choices for the present and future.

Chapter 2: Imaginative Generalization

1. An essay in *Discover* magazine offers a fascinating example with intriguing links to Whitehead's thought. Whitehead speculated that consciousness might have to do with how the biological processes of living cells change the properties of "empty space" inside the cells and in the brain. Recently, mathematical physicist Roger Penrose of Oxford University has teamed up with anesthesiologist Stuart Hameroff to explore the nature of consciousness. Hameroff suggests that "'consciousness under normal circumstances occurs at the level of space-time geometry in the brain, in the microtubules.' . . . 'But the fluctuations extend down to the Plank scale (far smaller than an atom).' . . . 'Penrose came up with a specific threshold that is conscious. He made the connection between the quantum possibilities in the universe and the quantum processes in the brain.' . . . 'I needed a mechanism, and he needed a structure, so we teamed up,' Hameroff says." From Jane Bosveld, "Soul Search," *Discover* (June 2007): 47–50.
2. In *Religion and Scientific Naturalism: Overcoming the Conflicts* (Albany, N.Y.: State University of New York Press, 2000), process philosopher and theolo-

gian David Ray Griffin distinguishes between "soft-core" common sense as the shared ideas of our culture and "hard-core" common sense as those beliefs that are necessarily presupposed by all rational thought, even where people consciously reject them. "Hard-core common sense" beliefs arise from universally shared experience and are "*inevitably presupposed in practice*" (99). These include at least: "(1) that we have conscious experience; (2) that this conscious experience, while influenced by our bodies, is not wholly determined thereby, but involves an element of self-determining freedom; and (3) that this partially free experience exerts efficacy upon our bodily behavior, giving us a degree of responsibility for our bodily actions" (137).

3. *The Bhagavad-Gita* (The Song of God), trans. Swami Prabhavananda and Christopher Isherwood (1944; repr., New York: Signet, 1972), 88–90. Citations are to the Signet edition.

Chapter 3: Minds, Bodies, and Experience

1. Thich Nhat Hanh, *The Heart of the Buddha's Teaching* (Berkeley, Calif.: Broadway Books, 1998), 121–22. There are strong connections between process thought and Buddhism. A fuller exploration of them lies beyond the scope of this book, but readers familiar with Buddhism will surely see many points of contact. For a good introduction, see John B. Cobb Jr., *Beyond Dialogue: Toward a Mutual Transformation of Christianity and Buddhism* (Philadelphia: Fortress Press, 1982).
2. *The Dialogues of Plato*, trans. Benjamin Jowett (New York: Random House, 1937), 2:12.
3. See David Ray Griffin, *Religion and Scientific Naturalism: Overcoming the Conflicts* (Albany, N.Y.: State University of New York Press, 2000), chapter 5. Griffin also describes other political and ecclesiastical motivations for this view.
4. Descartes proposed that the pineal gland somehow served as the link between mind and body, but clearly this proposal does not solve any of the problems described here. A later disciple of Descartes, Malebranche, recognizing that only supernatural intervention could solve the problem, proposed that God constantly worked miracles to provide the link. Perhaps that helped people to see how deep the problems in such dualism go.
5. I put the term *inside* in quotation marks to remind us how much this way of thinking harkens back to the idea of a little person being literally inside our head. What is trapped is the thinking brain in an otherwise nonfunctioning body.
6. René Descartes, *Discourse on Method, and Meditations on First Philosophy*, trans. Donald Cress (Indianapolis, Ind.: Hackett Publishing, 1980), 94–95.
7. "Correspondence with Princess Elisabeth, Concerning the Union of Mind and Body," in *The Essential Descartes*, ed. Margaret Wilson, reprinted in *Voices of Wisdom: A Multicultural Philosophy Reader*, ed. Gary E. Kessler, 4th ed. (Belmont, Calif.: Wadsworth, 2001), 532.
8. Manlio Argueta, *One Day of Life* (New York: Vintage, 1991), 20–21, 23, respectively.

9. Robert McAfee Brown, "Starting Over: New Beginning Points for Theology," *Christian Century* 97, no. 18 (May 14, 1980): 546.

Chapter 4: Experience All the Way Down

1. I fully appreciate and endorse the comment of Herman Greene and his wife Sandi that more enlightened animal training today involves "learning to think like the animal and rewarding good behavior." I'm better at that than I used to be, but I still have much to learn from my dogs.
2. For more on this, see Thomas Nagel, "What Is It Like to Be a Bat?" *The Philosophical Review* 83 (1974): 435–50.
3. Herman Greene, founding president of the International Process Network, reminds me that he and some other members of the process community would be more sympathetic to the ancient view that mountains and even rocks might have a higher level of experience than I am allowing here.
4. As with rocks, some process thinkers might argue that trees, while lacking brains, nevertheless have a high degree of internal relatedness that might make possible more unified experience than Whiteheadians generally expect.
5. David Ray Griffin, *Religion and Scientific Naturalism: Overcoming the Conflicts* (Albany, N.Y.: State University of New York Press, 2000), 176.
6. John Stuart Mill, *Utilitarianism*, ed. George Sher (Indianapolis, Ind.: Hackett Publishing Co., 1979), 12.

Chapter 5: Reality as Relational Process

1. René Descartes, *Philosophical Works of Descartes*, trans. Elizabeth Haldane and G. R. T. Ross (New York: Dover Publications, 1931), 1:232. Descartes was quick to point out that all created substances are dependent upon God, so, strictly speaking, only God would fully fit this definition of substance. Descartes would have us qualify the idea of created substances by saying that they exist independently except for their dependence on God.
2. David Hume, "Of Personal Identity," *A Treatise of Human Nature*, in *On Human Nature and the Understanding*, ed. Antony Flew (New York: Collier Books, 1962), 259.
3. Ibid., 258.
4. Ibid., 259.
5. Ibid., 261, 264.
6. René Descartes, *Discourse on Method and Meditations on First Philosophy*, trans. Donald Cress (Indianapolis, Ind.: Hackett Publishing, 1980), 63, 62, 61, respectively.
7. Whitehead, for example, like some middle Platonists, preserved Plato's forms. He called them "eternal objects"—possibilities—eternally envisaged by God. However, Whitehead rejected Plato's proposal that these forms constituted ultimate reality. The world of becoming and perishing is most fundamentally real.
8. *Society* is Whitehead's term. For further explanation, see *PR* 34 and the appendix "Getting Technical" to this book.

9. *The Bhagavad-Gita* (The Song of God), trans. Swami Prabhavananda and Christopher Isherwood (1944; repr., New York: Signet, 1972), 36–37. Citations are to the Signet edition.
10. John B. Cobb Jr. *Feminism and Process Thought* (Lewiston, N.Y.: Edwin Mellen Press, 1981), 53.
11. Descartes, *Philosophical Works*, 1:232.

Chapter 6: Reality as a Causal Web

1. David Hume, "Of the Idea of Necessary Connection," *An Inquiry concerning Human Understanding*, in *On Human Nature and the Understanding*, ed. Antony Flew (New York: Collier Books, 1962), 78.
2. Ibid., 88, 89.
3. Belief in causality would be an example of what David Griffin calls hard-core common sense. See n.2, chap.2, above. "Soft-core" common sense refers to the shared ideas of our culture and "hard-core" common sense to those beliefs that are necessarily presupposed by all rational thought, even where people consciously reject them. As Griffin explains, "hard-core common sense" beliefs arise from universally shared experience and are "*inevitably presupposed in practice*" (*Religion and Scientific Naturalism: Overcoming the Conflicts* [Albany, N.Y.: State University of New York Press, 2000], 99).

Chapter 7: Unilateral Power

1. Raymond Aron, *Peace and War: A Theory of International Relations*, trans. Richard Howard and Annette Baker Fos (New York and Washington: Frederick A. Praeger, 1967), 47.
2. Bernard Loomer, "Two Conceptions of Power," *Criterion* 15, no. 1 (Winter 1976): 7–29.
3. Plato, *The Sophist*, in *The Dialogues of Plato*, trans. Benjamin Jowett (New York: Random House, 1937), 2:255.
4. Plato, *The Republic*, in ibid., 1:645.
5. Plato, *The Timaeus*, in ibid., 2:12 (emphasis added).
6. René Descartes, *Philosophical Works of Descartes*, trans. Elizabeth Haldane and G. R. T. Ross (New York: Dover Publications, 1931), 1:239.
7. Gottfried Wilhelm Leibniz, *Leibniz: Discourse on Metaphysics/Correspondence with Arnauld/Monadology*, trans. George Montgomery (La Salle, Ill.: Open Court, 1973), 61–62.
8. John Locke, *An Essay Concerning Human Understanding*, ed. A.C. Fraser (New York: Dover Publications, 1959) 1:309–10.

Chapter 8: Relational Power

1. See Bernard Loomer, "Two Conceptions of Power," *Criterion* 15, no. 1 (Winter 1976): 7–29.
2. Ibid., 14.
3. Ibid., 16.

4. Ibid., 21.
5. Ibid., 29.
6. Ibid., 21.
7. Although this phrase is widely used and accepted now, I grow increasingly less comfortable with it, as it tends to suggest that "whites" are *not* people of color. Remember the old hymn: "Jesus loves the little children, all the children of the world, red and yellow, black and white, they are precious in his sight. . . ." Recently I saw it revised as " . . . shades of brown from dark to light. . . ." (Copyright, Community of Christ, 1997, adapted by Marge Nelson.) I paused in surprise, wondering about the change. Then I realized that the old color categories of red, yellow, black, and white must have been created to distinguish clearly the one superior, pure, white race from all the other "colored" races. I happily embraced the new wording. I am reminded by the old hymn that sometimes, even when we try hardest to speak out for loving equality, as the anonymous author of that old hymn surely did, we still work with the social language and concepts we have, which often carried unsuspected prejudices.
8. Inevitably, we are most motivated to be ecologically sensitive because the environment is essential to our own survival and our own humanity. But growth in relational sensitivity to that web leads to valuing other lives around us for their own sake because they have value to themselves, not merely because of their instrumental value for us.
9. John B. Cobb Jr., email to me, April 8, 2005.

Chapter 9: Creativity, Freedom, and God

1. Charles Hartshorne, *Creative Synthesis and Philosophic Method* (La Salle, Ill.: Open Court, 1970), 1, 2, 3, and 9, respectively. Italics in the original.
2. See the discussion of subjective aim in the appendix "Getting Technical" of this book for further discussion of the problem of freedom.

Chapter 10: Looking Ahead

1. *The Analects of Confucius: A Philosophical Translation*, trans. Roger T. Ames and Henry Rosemont Jr (New York: Ballantine Books, 1999), 23.
2. Ibid., 26. Italics in the original.
3. Ibid., 29.
4. *The Bhagavad-Gita* (The Song of God), trans. Swami Prabhavananda and Christopher Isherwood (1944; repr., New York: Signet, 1972), 61. Citations are to the Signet edition.
5. Ibid., 67.

Appendix: Getting Technical

1. For an alphabetical and more extensive glossary that is somewhat more technical than this, I strongly recommend Donald W. Sherburne, *A Key to Whitehead's Process and Reality* (Bloomington: Indiana University Press,

1966). I turned to Sherburne's glossary for thoughts on what should be covered here but have kept this appendix shorter and simpler than his work.

2. One effort to escape dualism is "emergentism," the view that experience emerges at some point in the biological evolutionary process, analogously to the way liquids emerge out of gases. I can see the appeal of this view. But water as H_2O surely builds on properties already existing in the two gases. How would this emergence create experience out of no experience *at all*? Thus, the analogy seems to Whiteheadians to fit better with the idea of awareness or consciousness emerging out of more primitive forms of experience.
3. I do not mean to suggest that the "relations" are something in addition to the actual entities. That would violate Whitehead's ontological principle. What holds the universe together is that actual entities experience other actual entities. That is what I mean here by relationships. A more adequate explanation would require a discussion of Whitehead's concept of the *extensive continuum* (see *PR* chapter 2).
4. We can, however, distinguish two senses of time. Primarily, there is the time that is the temporal experience of actual entities. However, we can also speak of time as the change from one occasion to the next, just as Whitehead speaks of change as the difference between successive occasions.
5. There are some technical issues I am avoiding here. If a star four light years away blows up, it will have no causal connection with us for four years because that is how long it takes light to get here. Thus, Whitehead spoke of contemporaries as events that do not interact causally because light travels at a finite speed. Recently, some experiments on simultaneous influence raise interesting new questions on these matters. It takes a moment for sound and light (scent, etc.) to reach you from the people and objects around you, even from your own nerves. So what is true of distant stars is also true of everything else.
6. Shortly afterward he added that " . . . we can say that God and the actual world jointly constitute the character of the creativity for the initial phase of the novel concrescence" (*PR* 245). It is a matter of some consequence to wonder whether the term "initial phase" in this second statement was intended to include—or ought to include—the "initial aim," since some process philosophers think that the world is capable of being the ground of freedom. But it seems clear that Whitehead did not share that view. He felt that God was essential as the locus of the novel possibilities necessary for actual entities to have some degree of freedom.
7. A principle point of discussion about whether Whitehead's vision of reality can work without God depends on whether the world itself can contain possibilities that have not yet been actualized. If it can, then Whitehead's argument for the role of God is undermined. Personally, being more of a nominalist, I think Whitehead's argument presupposes an excessively platonic view of possibilities.
8. There is obviously something of great theological import here. Whitehead gives clear meaning to the idea that God is omnipresent. At one level, revelation, providence, and the experience of divine caring would be radically

universalized. Process theology destroys all efforts to confine God's work, revelation, and love to a single community or tradition. As Herman Greene observed in an email comment, God as envisioned here "transcends any single community of people and any particular religious tradition while allowing each community and tradition to experience God as their own."

9. Plato, *The Sophist*, in *The Dialogues of Plato*, trans. Benjamin Jowett (New York: Random House, 1937), 2:255.
10. Martin Luther, *On the Bondage of the Will*, in *Luther and Erasmus: Free Will and Salvation*, trans. and ed. E. Gordon Rupp and Philip S. Watson, in collaboration with A. N. Marlow and B. Drewery (Philadelphia: Westminster Press, 1969), 139–40: "It means that the will cannot change itself and turn in a different direction. . . . By contrast, if God works in us, the will is changed. . . . Thus the human will is placed between the two like a beast of burden. If God rides it, it wills and goes where God wills. . . . If Satan rides it, it wills and goes where Satan wills; nor can it choose to run to either of the two riders or to seek him out. . . ."
11. Leibniz, *Monadology*, in *Leibniz: Discourse on Metaphysics/Correspondence with Arnauld/Monadolgy*, trans. George Montgomery (La Salle, Ill.: Open Court, 1973), 258 (#32).
12. This same idea is illustrated well in Charles Hartshorne's book, *Reality as Social Process* (New York: Hafner, 1971).
13. See, for example, David Ray Griffin, *Parapsychology, Philosophy, and Spirituality: A Postmodern Exploration* (Albany, N.Y.: SUNY Press, 1977).

Suggested Reading

While there are many excellent resources in process-relational theology, the primary motivation for my own book is the absence of truly introductory books in process-relational philosophy. Nevertheless, I offer a few suggestions here. Apart from my own brief introduction to process theology, this list is focused on Whitehead's philosophy and applications of it.

For more information contact the Center for Process Thought, 1325 N. College, Ave., Claremont, CA, 91711, (909-621-5330), ctr4process.org.

Applications of Whitehead's Thought

Mesle, C. Robert. *Process Theology: A Basic Introduction*. St. Louis, Mo.: Chalice Press, 1993.

Griffin, David, ed. *Founders of Constructive Postmodern Philosophy: Peirce, James, Bergson, Whitehead, and Hartshorne*. Albany, N.Y.: State University of New York Press, 1982. See especially John B. Cobb Jr.'s essay on Whitehead in this book. Along with Charles Hartshorne, John Cobb and David Griffin have been the most influential and prolific authors in the field of process-relational thought.

Griffin, David Ray. *Whitehead's Radically Different Postmodern Philosophy*. Albany, N.Y.: SUNY Press, 2007.

______. *Deep Religious Pluralism*. Louisville, Ky.: Westminster John Knox Press, 2005.

Daly, Herman E., and John B. Cobb Jr. *For the Common Good: Redirecting the Economy Toward Community, the Environment, and a Sustainable Future*. Boston: Beacon Press, 1989.

Cobb, John B. Jr., *A Christian Natural Theology*, 2nd ed. Louisville, Ky.: Westminster John Knox Press, 2007. This edition explores Whitehead's conceptuality more fully than the first edition, published in 1965.

McDaniel, Jay B. *With Roots and Wings: Christianity in an Age of Ecology and Dialogue*. Maryknoll, N.Y.: Orbis Books, 1995. Jay has several books using religious applications of process-relational thought to address issues of ecological and economic justice, religious pluralism, and related topics.

Brumbaugh, Robert. *Whitehead, Process Thought, and Education*. Albany, N.Y.: SUNY Press, 1982.

Allan, George, and Malcolm D. Evans, et al., eds. *A Different Three R's for Education: Reason, Relationality, Rhythm*. Amsterdam: Editions Rodopi B. V., 2006.

Kachappilly, Kurian. *Process: Implications and Applications*. Bangalore, India: Dharmaram Publications, 2006.

Selected Works by Whitehead

Whitehead, Alfred North. *Process and Reality*. Edited by David Ray Griffin and Donald W. Sherburne, corr. ed. New York: Free Press, 1978. Originally published in 1929.

———. *Modes of Thought*. New York: Free Press, 1937.

———. *Adventures of Ideas*. New York: Free Press, 1961. Originally published in 1933.

———. *Religion in the Making*. New York and Cleveland: World Publishing Company, 1971. Originally published in 1926.

Works on Whitehead's Philosophy

Hartshorne, Charles. *Whitehead's Philosophy*. Lincoln: University of Nebraska Press, 1972. Hartshorne was Whitehead's student and became one of his most influential interpreters, as well as developing his own approach to process-relational thought.

Hosinski, Thomas E. *Stubborn Fact and Creative Advance: An Introduction to the Metaphysics of Alfred North Whitehead*. Lanham, Md.: Rowman and Littlefield, 1993.

Sherburne, Donald W., ed. *A Key to Whitehead's Process and Reality*. Bloomington: Indiana University Press, 1966.

Kraus, Elizabeth M. *The Metaphysics of Experience: A Companion to Whitehead's Process and Reality*. New York: Fordham University Press, 1979.

Lowe, Victor. *Understanding Whitehead*. Baltimore, Md.: John Hopkins Press, 1962.

LeClerc, Victor. *Whitehead's Metaphysics*. Bloomington: Indiana University Press, 1975.

Index